"An excellent question-and-answer guide for anyone wanting to know the basics of Mormonism. Johanson's answers are direct, concise, and never misleading. They also *fairly* represent sincere, yet often critical, inquiries."

—Dr. Stephen Covey, author of *The 7 Habits of Highly Effective People*

"If everyone I met gave me three hours to talk with them about the Mormon Church, I'd do it. But because they don't, I'm planning to hand them a copy of Walker's book. It's easy to read, pleasantly conversational, and a refreshingly clear explanation of Mormonism for those who are curious about The Church of Jesus Christ of Latter-day Saints, but don't know who to ask."

—Bill Marriott, CEO of Marriott International

"When its editors sent us this book for endorsement, we were wary . . . because writing a book of simple yet accurate answers to religious questions is not easy! But Johanson won us over. His answers are clear and balanced . . . and generally right on."

—Richard and Linda Eyre, *The New York Times* #1 bestselling authors of *Teaching Your Children Values* and *The Happy Family*

What Is
Mormonism
All About?

*Answers to the 150 Most
Commonly Asked Questions
About The Church of Jesus
Christ of Latter-day Saints*

W. F. Walker Johanson

 ST. MARTIN'S GRIFFIN ❧ NEW YORK

ISBN 0-312-28962-6

10 9 8 7 6 5

To my beloved wife, Kerry, and to our terrific children, Nils, Cooper (and husband Ben), Håkon, Riley, and Carson

CONTENTS

ACKNOWLEDGMENTS

I would like to thank my wife, Kerry, for putting up with me for all these years. Most of what I've learned in this life—that's of lasting value—I've learned from her. I would also like to thank my good friend and brother-in-the-Gospel, Roger Bradford, for his proofing assistance and for his treasured friendship.

FOREWORD

This coming February, the world's attention will be riveted on Salt Lake City, Utah, for the Winter Olympic Games. No doubt many people have heard of Utah's majestic mountains; its world-renowned national parks; and of course, "Mormons"—the popular nickname for members of The Church of Jesus Christ of Latter-day Saints. But there are probably few that understand much about the Church—its doctrine, the fascinating story behind its establishment, or its growing influence around the world.

The tens of thousands of visitors expected to visit our great state this winter, and the resulting media focus on Utah and its Olympic Games, will spark a great deal more interest in The Church of Jesus Christ, which is now the fastest growing religion in the Americas and perhaps the world.

Walker Johanson, a convert to the Church with a keen insight into its doctrines and culture, has anticipated many of the questions that visitors and fans of the Olympics are bound to ask themselves. Through the years, Walker has made something of a personal hobby out of gathering some of the most commonly asked questions about the Church. Now, he has used that material to create this highly informative and very interesting book that will help members and non-members alike understand a great deal more about what "Mormons" are all about. The book is a concise, informative, timely, and very interesting look at The Church of Jesus Christ of Latter-day Saints.

In its seventeen chapters, which are organized by categories of commonly asked questions, readers will find humor, insights into the Church's doctrine, and Walker's personal explanations for some of the unique characteristics of "Mormon" lifestyle, culture, and interest in family history. Walker also introduces readers to some of the more famous members who are entertainers, athletes, CEOs, and politicians.

Everyone coming to Utah—or who has a curiosity about our Church—will find this book invaluable. I have found it to be extremely interesting, and recommend it to everyone who's curious about why The Church of Jesus Christ of Latter-day Saints is one of the world's fastest growing religions.

Senator Orrin Hatch
Washington, D.C.

August 15, 2001

INTRODUCTION

I'm a University of Michigan graduate. And, like most Michigan grads, I'm a big football fan (so much so, that we even had a license plate once that read "Bo Schem"). Sometimes I'll wear a little gold block M lapel pin on my suit coat to show my allegiance. Invariably, wherever I am when I'm wearing that pin (even if I'm on a plane between Marseilles and Amsterdam), someone will either say: "Go Blue" (the universal Michigan welcome), or "Boo Michigan" (if they happen to be an Ohio State or a Notre Dame fan). It's uncanny. That little block M is instantly recognized around the world.

But the same isn't true for Mormons. Although there are more than 11 million Mormons around the world (and only about 300,000 Michigan alums), you never really know who, in any crowd, might be a member of The Church of Jesus Christ of Latter-day Saints. Sure, you can spot the Mormon missionaries in their white shirts and ties, and little black name tags (the "bicycle guys," as a business contact recently referred to them), but there's no way of knowing who, among all the people you might cross paths with on any given day, is a Mormon.

This book was written to help those of you who are curious about Mormons and their beliefs—and who may have many misconceptions and misinformation about Mormonism—by answering those questions that you have mulling around in your head . . . that you've been reluctant to voice, out of fear of being "pounced on" by the nearest pair of Mormon missionaries.

Your interest may be simple curiosity; it may be because a friend or relative became a Mormon, and you wonder why; it may be because the Olympics are on TV, and they're constantly showing pictures of the Mormon temple and the Tabernacle Choir; it may be because your minister mentioned Mormonism in a sermon; or it may be because you're searching for something that's missing in your life . . . and you want to check out all the options.

This book was written for you. It's not complicated; it's not hard to read or understand; it's not too deep or scholarly. Rather, it was written to answer both your lighthearted and your serious questions, to correct any common misperceptions, to "demystify" the myths, and to help you get a clearer understanding of what Mormonism is all about. You don't even need to read it all. You can merely flip through it . . . looking for those questions that are of particular interest to you.

But my hope is that, after reading it, you'll be much more comfortable in approaching those Mormons you know (neighbors, friends, relatives, co-workers, classmates, and so on) . . . and asking them the questions that are still on your mind, that maybe I've neglected to answer in this book.

1 ARE MORMONS CHRISTIAN? WHAT DO THEY THINK OF JESUS CHRIST?

Q *Are Mormons Christians?*

Mormonism is a Christian religion. Mormons believe in Jesus of Nazareth, and consider Him to be the Son of God and the Savior of the world. At Baptism, Mormons take upon themselves the name of Jesus Christ, so as to be counted among His followers. They believe that Jesus Christ is the one and only route to salvation, and therefore they proudly proclaim themselves to be Christians.

However, they are not Protestants, and this is a point of confusion among many non-Mormons. Here's how Mormons can consider themselves Christians but not Protestants:

At the time of Christ, the people in the area around Jerusalem were mostly Palestinians, Romans, or Jews, and those who followed Christ were labeled Christians. Several hundred years after the Crucifixion and Resurrection of Jesus (and the death of the Apostles), the Catholic Church was formed, claiming that it represented the continuation of the Christian faith. The word *Catholic* in Latin means "universal," so it claimed to represent the universal Christian Church.

Aside from other splits that had occurred, the Catholic Church was "The Church" in Western Europe until the time of Martin Luther, who was a Catholic who split away from the Church and formed his own version of Christianity, which came to be called Lutheranism. This was the beginning of the reform movement in Christianity, now called the Reformation. Soon others also began to split off from the Catholic Church, and they were all called Protestant denominations, because they "protested" the accuracy and correctness of the Catholic Church, as representing Christ's true church. So all subsequent Christian faiths were considered to be Protestant, as opposed to Catholic.

But among Mormons, the source of their church was not as a spin-off from Catholicism or another Protestant denomination, but they allege that a young fourteen-year-old boy was "called" by God to be a prophet (as were Abraham and Moses of old), and given the charge to restore Christ's original Church to the earth. This boy's name was Joseph Smith Jr. He was born in 1805, lived in Upstate New York (in the newly established United States of America), and Mormons believe that he was visited by God the Father and His Son, Jesus Christ (and subsequently by other angels from heaven), who instructed him on how to restore the true Church of Jesus Christ. This is how Mormons claim to be Christians, without considering themselves Protestants.

Q Do Mormons worship someone named Mormon?

Mormons do not worship someone named Mormon. The term *Mormon* comes from the engraved plates that Mormons believe were written by ancient prophets of God, from 600 B.C. to 400 A.D. (who themselves were Christians), that were found, under God's direction, by Joseph Smith in Upstate New York in 1824. The translated record from those plates is entitled the *Book of Mormon,* because a man named Mormon was one of the last prophets to write on them.

Mormons believe the Book of Mormon to be Scripture, the same as they believe the Holy Bible—both the Old and New Testaments—to be Scripture. Because early anti-Mormons didn't understand these facts, they assumed that Mormons must worship somebody named Mormon, and tried to mock them by calling them "Mormons." Mormons don't worship the prophet Mormon any more than the Jews worship the prophet Moses. They look up to him, they admire him, they consider him a beloved prophet; but he is not a god, he is but a prophet of Jesus Christ.

Q *Why do Mormons call themselves Mormons?*

The truth of the matter is that Mormons don't call themselves Mormons. The term *Mormon* was originally used by anti-Mormons in the 1830s, '40s, and '50s, to taunt and poke fun at the members of The Church of Jesus Christ of Latter-day Saints. It was intended as a term of mockery, derision, and hatred. But rather than being offended, Mormons eventually accepted the term, and now are happily willing to call themselves Mormons. (However, to help clarify their status as a Christian denomination, Church officials are currently encouraging members to refer to themselves as "members of The Church of Jesus Christ of Latter-day Saints," and to minimize the use of the term *Mormon* where possible.)

Q *Do Mormons believe in the Trinity?*

For nearly two thousand years, the Christian world has used the term *the Trinity* to refer to the Godhead, made up of God the Father, His Son Jesus Christ, and the Holy Ghost. All of Christianity has long believed that the Trinity represented the three somewhat different but overlapping functions of one eternal God.

Mormons, on the other hand, believe that when Joseph Smith prayed for guidance about which church to join, that God the Father and Jesus Christ both visited him, and that when he viewed them, they were two separate "personages" (a term that Mormons use to indicate that they were two separate entities, but not "people," so as not to have detractors claim that Mormons believe that God and Jesus are just "people"), just like they were when Stephen saw them (see Acts 7:55–56).

Joseph Smith claimed that they told him (in addition to other teachings they gave him at that time) that the prevailing Christian view of the Trinity (representing three functions in one God) was erroneous, and that, in truth, the three members of the Godhead were three separate personages. Mormons, therefore, believe that in heaven there is God the Father, His Son Jesus Christ (whom Mormons believe was Jehovah of the Old Testament, but who, when He was born in Bethlehem to Mary, was renamed Jesus of Nazareth—the long-awaited Jewish Messiah [the Greek word is *Christ*]), and the Holy Ghost.

The Mormon understanding of the Trinity is that these are three distinct personages in the Godhead. The non-Mormon Christian world believes that—in some miraculous way—these three represent the same God, while

Mormons believe that they represent individual personages as a part of the eternal plan of God. As Mormons would say: "When Jesus prays to Heavenly Father, He is praying to His actual father, He is not praying to Himself." For Mormons, this makes a lot of sense, and is a normal, wonderful, and refreshingly rational explanation. But for some non-Mormons, this is a very heretical, blasphemous, and offensive view, which contributes to anti-Mormon sentiment among some fundamentalist Christian groups.

Q Isn't it true that the real name of the Mormon Church is "The Church of Latter Day Saints"?

When the Mormon Church is mentioned in the media, it is often referred to as "The Church of Latter Day Saints." This is entirely incorrect.

Why the media calls it this is a little baffling, but it is probably due to one of the following two explanations:

1. Many media people may be unaware that the Mormon Church's real name is The Church of Jesus Christ of Latter-day Saints. Or, when they research what term to use, they go to sources other than the Mormon Church—which may intentionally give them erroneous information.

-or-

2. Because some media outlets may be afraid of hostile backlash from some fundamentalist Christian groups who don't consider Mormons to be Christians, and who don't want the public persuaded into thinking that maybe Mormons really *are* Christians . . . these media outlets may intentionally "avoid" inserting the "Jesus Christ" portion of the Mormon Church's real name.

And although Mormons typically don't even notice, or don't particularly mind, the incorrect term, there is no such church as "The Church of Latter Day Saints." The fact is that Mormons are faithful believers in Jesus Christ, and consider themselves committed Christians. The official name of the Mormon Church is The Church of Jesus Christ of Latter-day Saints, and Mormons would prefer that everyone call it that.

Q Do Mormons believe that Jesus Christ is the Savior of the world?

Yes. Mormons believe that there is only one God the Father, and they typically refer to Him as "Heavenly Father." They believe that Jesus of Nazareth is the literal Son of God and is the only one with the title of Christ, and therefore the Savior of all mankind—and the only way by which mankind can be saved. In their view, this makes them Christians. They believe in Christ; they believe that Jesus is *the* Christ; and they take seriously their belief that the path that Jesus taught in the Scriptures, is the only way back to God the Father, in the Celestial Kingdom of heaven. They share the view of all Christendom that there is no other way by which man may be saved, except through the Lord Jesus Christ. They are strong believers in Jesus Christ and His teachings in the New Testament; and they believe that the teachings of the Book of Mormon go hand-in-hand with the teachings of the New Testament (in fact, the subtitle of the Book of Mormon is "Another Testament of Jesus Christ").

There are those who are hostile to the Mormon Church, who claim that Mormons worship Joseph Smith. This is not so. There are those who claim that Mormons worship Mormon. This is not so. There are those who claim that Mormons do not worship Jesus Christ and therefore are not Christians. This is certainly not so, as Mormons are committed, dedicated Christians who see themselves as having been "born again" at Baptism, and as taking upon themselves the name of Jesus Christ, and who believe that there is no other way to salvation except through the grace and Atonement, sacrifice and Resurrection of the Lord Jesus Christ.

Q Whom do Mormons pray to?

As Christians, Mormons are a praying people, who direct their prayers only to God the Father. And because they believe that Jesus is our advocate with God the Father, they close all of their prayers by saying: ". . . in the name of Jesus Christ, Amen." To reiterate, Mormons do not pray to Jesus (they pray in His name to God the Father); they do not pray to Joseph Smith, to the prophet Mormon, or to anyone other than God the Father.

2 IS THE BOOK OF MORMON THEIR BIBLE? WHAT DO MORMONS THINK OF THE BIBLE?

Q *Do Mormons believe in the Bible?*

Yes. Mormons accept both the Old Testament and the New Testament as the Word of God. They teach both in their Sunday Schools; their teenagers learn both in their seminary classes; and they have courses in both the Old and New Testaments in their colleges and universities. Mormons are strong believers in the Holy Bible; and they use the *King James Version* exclusively.

In fact, most Mormons know a lot more about the Old and New Testaments than do most casual Protestants and Catholics. They see the Old Testament as the scriptural record of the holy prophets sent from God the Father to teach His children the truths of the Gospel Plan of Salvation as it would be taught by Jesus Christ, when He arrives. (In fact, Mormons believe that the Jehovah of the Old Testament *is* the premortal Jesus Christ of the New Testament. And that Jehovah is Jesus' name in heaven, prior to His being born on this earth. The word *Jesus*, as is taught in the New Testament, means "God with us." Jehovah *with* the people on earth.)

Mormons revere the New Testament as well. For truly they see it as the record of the birth, life, teachings, death, and Resurrection of the Lord and Savior, Jesus Christ, as well as the stories of His beloved disciples (the Twelve Apostles) after His death. Interestingly enough, the Mormon Church is the only church that currently claims to have a prophet and Twelve Apostles, just as the primitive Church under Jesus Christ had during the meridian of time. (And for those Christians who feel that there are some obscure passages in Revelation and Isaiah, for instance, and in other parts of both the Old and New Testaments, you would be fascinated to read some of the detailed scholarly commentaries by Mormon authors on those books. Most people are unaware of these commentaries, because "Christian" bookstores don't inventory Mormon scholarly publications, for they view them as false and un-Christian. The only Mormon-related materials in most Christian bookstores are anti-Mormon materials.)

Q *Why do the Mormons talk so much about the Book of Mormon? If they're Christians, why don't they just use the Bible?*

Mormons do use the Bible. And it's not that Mormons decided that they wanted a Book of Mormon. The fact is that it was the Book of Mormon that convinced the early believers that the boy Joseph Smith was a prophet, who had been called by God to restore the original Church of Jesus Christ.

Most of the early Mormons had previously been members of other Protestant denominations. They believed in the Bible, and were not looking for any Scripture beyond what was in the Bible.

However, Mormons believe that God led Joseph Smith to a hillside in northern New York State, in which was buried (1,400 years earlier), thin metal plates of gold and brass, on which were inscribed the sacred records of prophets who had lived on the American continent. These were new writings that, to Mormons, represented additional Sacred Scriptures that supplement those in the Bible—and teach the exact same principles.

Mormons agree with the teachings in the Bible, and only rely on additional teachings where Biblical records that had been written are now lost or have not been included in either the Old or New Testament. Mormons see the Book of Mormon as helping to clarify some of the more confusing or incomplete passages from the Bible, and, in fact believe that one of the reasons God called Joseph Smith to find and publish the Book of Mormon records is because the prophets of God in the New World retained their records more carefully than did the Apostles of Christ's time in the Old World, and that not all of Paul's letters are available, but that if they were all found, they would merely reinforce the exact same teachings that are found in the Book of Mormon.

The Bible, as we know it, represents the compilations of the words of various prophets, as selected and edited by the fourth- and fifth-century leaders of the Catholic Church. Even then, there were prophets whose writings were left out of the Bible, there were prophets whose writings were not found, and there were prophets whose writings were modified to keep them in agreement with what the early Christian and secular leaders wanted to establish.

Mormons believe that the Book of Mormon helps Christians understand the Bible better. They didn't decide that they wanted a Book of Mormon, rather they were presented with the Book of Mormon, and declare that they've gained a testimony that it is truly a sacred record of the words of previously unknown prophets of God; and that it serves as a valuable supplement to the Holy Bible, and as a "second witness" to the divinity of Jesus Christ. Therefore, they do not criticize other Christians for relying solely on the Bible, they merely encourage people to read the Book of Mormon, too, for they assert that it supports, strengthens, expands, and helps to clarify some of the more confusing portions of the Bible.

Q *What is the Book of Mormon about?*

Mormons claim that the Book of Mormon is a compilation of the written records of many different prophets of God, starting with a Jewish prophet named Lehi, who lived in Jerusalem in 600 B.C., who was told by God to take his family out of Jerusalem—with copies of the Old Testament as they had at that time—and to flee into the wilderness, because Jerusalem was soon to be overrun and all the Jews killed or taken captive into Babylon.

Lehi and his family traveled in the wilderness for several years, and were eventually directed to build a ship and sail it to what is now Central America in the western hemisphere. Soon after their arrival in this "Promised Land," Lehi's sons split in anger into two main tribes or camps. One group followed the eldest son, whose name was Laman, and they became known as Lamanites. The other group followed another son, whose name was Nephi, and they became known as Nephites.

The Book of Mormon recounts the history of these peoples—and their expansion, their civilization, their wars, their evils, their periods of repentance and righteousness, and the words of the holy prophets that God sends to them over the thousand-year period between 600 B.C. and approximately 400 A.D. It includes a visit of the Lord Jesus Christ to the American continent, soon after His Resurrection from the Holy Land, and His teachings, face-to-face, with the people of Book of Mormon times. (Mormons believe that many of these same people are the ancestors of the Native American Indians of today.)

In time, the wicked Lamanite tribes overran the righteous

Nephite tribes, and the last two surviving righteous people were a prophet whose name was Mormon, and his son, Moroni. All of the sacred writings of the prophets, from Lehi to the present, had been passed down to Mormon by previous prophets. But because there were so many records, Mormon, after reading them all, inscribed a consolidated version upon plates of gold and brass, which he gave to his son, Moroni, upon his death. And under the direction of God, Moroni buried these records in a stone box in the side of a hill, where they lay hidden for those 1,400 years, until God sent this same Moroni (now in angelic form) to Joseph Smith to find them, and make available the teachings of these prophets to the world.

Because of this miraculous (and some say far-fetched) story (although Mormons will counter that it's no more far-fetched than the story of Jesus' Resurrection), Mormons believe that the New World was intentionally kept hidden by God from the European and Asian civilizations, until after the Reformation and the Protestant era had begun, whereupon it would be discovered just in time for those fleeing religious persecution to be led to a land where they could be free to worship in a way they would like to (i.e., the Pilgrims).

Mormons see a grand scheme in all of this, orchestrated by God. They see the discovery of the New World and the establishment of the United States of America as all being a part of God's plan to create a new nation that, at that time, would be the only nation on earth that—because of its new democratic principles and constitutionally protected freedom of religion—would permit a "new religion" to safely be established. In those days, if a new religion had been formed in France or England, or Russia or China, it would have been outlawed and destroyed. But in America, where there was freedom of religion, a new religion had the opportunity to be established.

And so Mormons believe that God intentionally withheld discovery of America from the rest of the European world until the timing was right, for those fleeing to the colonies in pursuit of religious freedom were the forerunners of the founders of a nation that permitted freedom of religion, which would ultimately allow the restoration of the original Church of Jesus Christ. Mormons believe that Joseph Smith's birth soon after the founding of the United States, and his inquiring into which church to join, were all a part of God's plan to permit the restoration of both the records from the prophet Mormon, and also the restoration of Christ's Church in an environment where it would be permitted to grow from a very small seed.

There were only six members when the Mormon Church was established in 1830, and there are more than 11 million members worldwide, as of 2001.

Q *Most people think the Old Testament is about the Jews, and the New Testament is about Jesus. What do Mormons think?*

While most people see the Old Testament as about the Jews, and the New Testament as about Jesus, Mormons have quite a different view. They view the Old Testament as the record of the prophets of God who lived on the earth before Jesus was born, but who taught Christianity and the basic principles of the Gospel of Jesus Christ. The Mormon interpretation is that the people in Old Testament times were not as obedient to His counsel as He had hoped, so He sent Moses as a prophet to give them a stricter version of the Gospel of Jesus Christ, called the Law of Moses, which was based on the Ten Commandments.

The Law of Moses was a stricter version, because the people seemed unwilling and unable to live the more Christ-like "charitable" version, and they were also taught the law of sacrifice, which was a precursor to the future sacrifice of God's only begotten Son, the Lord Jesus Christ.

To Mormons, therefore, when Jesus Christ Himself gave His own life as an atonement for the sins of mankind, this sacrifice of the Lamb of God represented the culmination of the Law of Moses, and the reintroduction of the basic principles of the Gospel of Jesus Christ. Instead of the Law of Moses' "eye for an eye," it was the Gospel of Jesus Christ's "love your neighbor."

And, therefore, Mormons see the Old Testament as God's word to His people before Christ's birth, the New Testament as God's word to His people during Christ's life on earth (and the subsequent time, primarily through the teachings of the Apostle Paul), and the Book of Mormon as God's word to His people in the western hemisphere.

The Book of Mormon is the story of Old Testament prophets who were led by God to sail to the New World, and their writings record the visit of Jesus Christ to the people in the western hemisphere immediately after His Resurrection in the Old World of Jerusalem. Mormons believe that just as Jesus had revealed Himself to His disciples and others in Palestine after His Resurrection, He also visited the people in the New World (see John 10:16). To Mormons, the record of that visit is included in the Book of Mormon; and the Book of Mormon is, to them, merely another book of Scripture written by God's prophets about Jesus Christ; about God's teachings before Jesus was born; about Jesus' teachings when He was on the earth; and about the teachings of the prophets and the Apostles who were called in the New World, just as they were in the Old World—like Paul, who taught the Gospel, who held the priesthood of God, who was an Apostle of the Lord Jesus Christ, who wrote His inspired teachings down—and that those are the very teachings that also appear in the Book of Mormon.

And so, from the Mormon perspective, the Book of Mormon is merely another body of accurately recorded Scripture to supplement the Old Testament and the New Testament. And Mormons even believe that when the ten lost tribes of Israel are rediscovered, there will be additional records—like those that constitute the Book of Mormon—that had been kept by worthy prophets in those areas, that will yet be added to the body of Holy Scripture.

Q Who is Mormon, and why was the book named after him?

The Book of Mormon represents the writings of many of God's prophets from about 600 B.C. to 400 A.D., representing a thousand years, or forty to fifty generations of people. Mormons believe that, as with the Bible, prophets would write their observations, store them, hand them down to subsequent prophets, and eventually die. Some of those writings inevitably became lost; and many of those writings became voluminous and heavy, as they were often inscribed on brass or gold panels, for permanence.

Near the end of the time covered in the Book of Mormon, the next to the last prophet's name was Mormon. He was one of the last remaining members of his tribe, all of whom had been killed through iniquity, wars, and bloodshed. As a prophet, he had access to the location of all of these old sacred writings, and spent many of his last years compiling, editing, and abridging those records so that he could carry them more readily. It was his son, Moroni, to whom he gave his abridgment of those writings before he died.

Moroni is then the one, Mormons believe, who buried these final compilations in a stone box, under the ground, on a hillside—the same hillside where, in 1824, Joseph Smith found them. Mormons claim that Joseph Smith was led to that spot by an angel, and that the angel was that same Moroni who buried the plates 1,400 years earlier. They assert that after Moroni died and returned to heaven he was then given the assignment to visit the boy Joseph Smith and lead him to where he had buried the sacred records.

The records became known as the Book of Mormon because, when Joseph began translating the engraved plates into English through the power of God, the translation revealed that the record was the abridged book that had been compiled by the prophet Mormon. It is, however, made up of selections that Mormon compiled from the earlier writings of many other prophets, so the title merely indicates that the book was put together by Mormon, although it represents the writings of many dozens of prophets and is organized by prophet name into fifteen different books within the Book of Mormon that are all organized by chapter and verse, just like they are in the Bible.

Mormons believe that the prophet Mormon was a Christian; they claim that he was a prophet of the Lord Jesus Christ; that he taught the same principles of the Gospel that Adam taught, that Noah taught, that Abraham taught, that Moses taught, that Jesus taught, that the Apostle Paul taught, and that Joseph Smith taught.

Q *Is the Book of Mormon just made up by somebody? Or is there any evidence that it might be what Mormons claim it is?*

The small group of antagonists of the Church vehemently claims that the Book of Mormon was just made up by Joseph Smith—that it was a hoax from the beginning, and that it continues to be perpetrated today. However, millions of Mormons will unapologetically bear their testimony of the divinity of the Book of Mormon. However remarkable the story sounds, Mormons claim it to be true.

Now, there are those—both in and out of the Church—who have sought physical evidence to either prove or disprove the claims made by Joseph Smith.

Joseph Smith reported that, after the translation was completed, angels came and took the original plates away, so that the plates are no longer on the earth. Mormons take this explanation at face value; anti-Mormons scoff at this "convenient" assertion. However, Joseph Smith was not the only one who claimed to have seen and handled the golden plates. There were eleven others who were shown the plates by Joseph, and these men signed written statements (which are reprinted at the beginning of the Book of Mormon), saying that they physically saw and handled the gold plates. Even though several of these people eventually left the Church, none of them ever recanted their testimonies. For believers, these eyewitness accounts serve as evidence. For nonbelievers, they only see a conspiracy to perpetuate the hoax.

Whether or not Joseph Smith was telling the truth is one of the key issues that people must carefully consider as they decide whether or not to join the Mormon Church, because there is no hard evidence one way or another. But Mormons would add: "Isn't that why faith is required? Doesn't it take faith to believe the stories about Jesus? Did Joseph Smith teach anything other than to believe in Jesus Christ? Why is seeing Joseph Smith as a servant of Jesus Christ so difficult?"

Furthermore, Mormons have gathered volumes of information to show that an uneducated fourteen-year-old boy, in Upstate New York in the 1820s, could not possibly have fabricated this document. The translation of the Book of Mormon took about six months. Mormons claim that, through inspiration from God, Joseph Smith translated the engravings, and dictated them for a scribe to write down verbatim. He did not go back; he did not edit; he read the engravings aloud, line after line; and he could start in mid-sentence, even after several days had gone by since his last translation session.

Recent scholarship has tested and retested the manuscript, looking for errors and inconsistencies, but none have been found. In fact, there is even evidence that some of the phrasing and terminology from the Book of Mormon follows patterns of similar phrasing and terminology from ancient documents discovered only recently, which Joseph Smith, of course, could not possibly have known. There are even discernible, measurable, and computer-analyzed patterns of speech that are unique to the different prophets whose writing appear in the Book of Mormon, which Joseph Smith would have been totally incapable of fabricating. Clearly, there is as much circumstantial evidence in favor of Joseph Smith *not* being able to make up the Book of Mormon, as there are assertions, among his detractors, that he did.

Q Are there any archeological sites that have either proven or disproven parts of the Book of Mormon?

There are many archeologists who have made (and are continuing to make) efforts to find the locations in Central and South America that are described in the Book of Mormon, to see if indeed some of those places actually existed. There are many books that have been written that claim that such evidence has been found, and others that claim that the possible link to Book of Mormon claims is unsubstantiated.

Many Mormons, however, feel that the search for such evidence misses the point. They point to Jesus' teachings about those who are always looking for a "sign," or a *proof* that God lives or that Jesus is really the Son of God. He points out that those who look for such signs have no faith, and are not believers.

Throughout history, people have looked for hard evidence—a splinter from the Cross at Calvary; a piece of leather from one of the Apostle Paul's sandals; the Ark of the Covenant; the Holy Grail; the Shroud of Turin. These are the same kinds of evidence that both believers and detractors have sought for centuries.

Mormons, however, believe that God will intentionally *withhold* such hard evidence from mankind, just to test (or "prove") their faith. Mormons believe that Jesus taught that by faith they must live, that by faith they will be tried and tested, and that by faith they must make their choice to join or not to join, to follow or not to follow, to believe or not to believe, to obey or not to obey. They believe that the presence of hard evidence would supplant the need for such faith, and therefore they feel that it is God's plan that such evidence will not be available, just so believers will be forced to make their decision on the basis of faith, and

23

nonbelievers will be held accountable for whether or not they choose to exercise such faith. From this perspective, the long-term desirability of ever having such hard evidence—until Jesus Himself returns at the time of the Second Coming—is not needed by most Mormons in order for them to believe.

Q *So how is anyone supposed to determine whether or not the Book of Mormon is a true book of Scripture?*

Nearly all religions claim that the only way to know what's true is to exercise faith. But for many people, that's a nebulous concept that's way out-of-sync with the highly organized rational approaches that define the thinking man or woman of the twenty-first century. Furthermore, when we observe people who are overtly religious, we often perceive them as "different," as "weird," as "not like the kind of people I hang around with," or even like they're faking it.

What's different about the Mormons is that they never expect you to take their word for it. They don't expect you to believe what they're saying just because they're nice, or just because they're "really sincere." They actually have a way for each person investigating Mormonism to find out for him or herself if the Book of Mormon is a true book of Holy Scripture, and if The Church of Jesus Christ of Latter-day Saints is Christ's true Church.

In Mormonism's case, no one ever has to be persuaded by some Church member to join the Church. That's because the Book of Mormon has a built-in device for determining whether or not these things are true. Here's how Mormons claim it works:

1. The curious investigator needs to read the Book of Mormon.

2. Upon completion of the book, the reader then needs to ask God, in private and direct prayer, for an answer to his or her questions about what is

true, as outlined in the following verses from near the end of the Book of Mormon:

Behold, I would exhort you that when ye shall read these things, if it be wisdom in God that ye should read them, that ye would remember how merciful the Lord hath been unto the children of men, from the creation of Adam even down until the time that ye shall receive these things, and ponder it in your hearts.

And when ye shall receive these things, I would exhort you that ye would ask God, the Eternal Father, in the name of Christ, if these things are not true; and if ye shall ask with a sincere heart, with real intent, having faith in Christ, he will manifest the truth of it unto you, by the power of the Holy Ghost.

And by the power of the Holy Ghost ye may know the truth of all things.

—Moroni 10:3–5

3 HOW IS MORMONISM DIFFERENT FROM OTHER RELIGIONS (INCLUDING MORMONISM'S AFFINITY FOR THE JEWS)?

Q *What's the difference between Protestant denominations and the Mormons?*

Although many practicing and faithful Christians are unaware of these historical facts, the Catholic Church was the primary organization that claimed that, through the Apostle Peter, it had the authority to represent the Church that Jesus Christ established. *Catholic* is the Latin word for "universal," so the Catholic Church merely meant the universal Church, patterned after what they felt Jesus had taught.

However, the Catholic Church, in its early iterations, was also a political organization. In Rome, the Catholic Church ran the government (and much of Western Europe). And there are many histories that portray how some of these early Church leaders were not true believers, were ruthless power brokers, and were not Christ-like in their behavior; although, of course, there were also many early Catholic leaders who were very Christ-like, very charitable, and very righteous.

But the Catholic Church, as it evolved, was a combination of both a political government and an attempt to represent the Church as Jesus had established it. It was some of these early Catholics who selected the books to be included in the Bible. But they did not include all of the scriptural sources that were available; and they modified some of the others, so that the early versions of the Hebrew and Greek Bibles, as organized by the Catholic Church, represented a selection of what best fit what the Church leaders wanted to teach.

As Europe continued through the Dark Ages, into the Middle Ages, and toward the Renaissance, there were those Catholics who began to look back at the history of the Catholic Church and felt that there were errors introduced; that there were practices that were not the original practices; and that there were those who were unrighteous in their leadership.

One of the foremost of these concerned Church members was Martin Luther, a German Catholic who was the first of the Protestant Reformers. He proposed that the Church had gone astray on several points, and suggested that the Church should correct its doctrine to be more in line with what he felt were Christ's original teachings. The Catholic hierarchy, of course, called his suggestions blasphemy, and excommunicated him. He then proceeded to establish his own church, which he claimed was a return to the principles that Jesus had taught.

Martin Luther was the first of many Protestants, or "protestors," to the Catholic Church. Luther was one; John Wesley was another; John Calvin was another; and there were many others who attempted to reestablish—as best they could—the Church that Jesus Himself had established. Therefore, most Christian denominations in the world today are either various forms of Catholicism (such as the

Roman Catholics; the Eastern Orthodox Church, which represents the Eastern European version of Roman Catholicism; the Anglican Church, which was the United Kingdom's version of Catholicism when Henry VIII requested a divorce and the Roman Catholic Church wouldn't honor it, so he just disbanded it and reestablished it as the Church of England with his own leaders; and the Episcopal Church, the Colonial American version of the Anglican Church), or they are one of the many Protestant denominations—the Lutherans, the Methodists, the Presbyterians, the Baptists, the Congregationalists, the Quakers, the Dutch Reformed, the Mennonites, the Amish, and all of the many other Protestant spin-off groups—among which were the Pilgrims, who fled religious persecution to the New World, America, where they sought to practice their interpretation of original Christianity within the freedom from political persecution that the New World provided.

With this background, nearly all Christian denominations are either from the Catholic model or the Protestant model, in one form or another. There are, however, some who have claimed visions or revelations, and who have established churches from scratch. They have often taken components of these other versions, but have interpreted them for themselves. These include Mary Baker Eddy's establishment of Christian Science, the Shakers, and other groups, which have attempted to reestablish the original primitive Church that Christ had established.

Among this group are the Mormons. While never intending to start his own church, Joseph Smith claimed that he prayed to God for guidance about which church he should join, and God the Father appeared to him with Jesus Christ, and answered his question by saying something like: "Don't join any of them . . . none of them are my true

Church. But if you remain righteous, I will use you as an instrument in my hands to restore my true Church."

From this perspective, Mormons claim that their church is a "restored" Christian church, rather than a derivative of either the Catholic or the Protestant models.

Q *What do Mormons think of Calvin, or Wesley, or Mohammed, or Martin Luther, or the Pope?*

The Mormon view is that these were all wonderfully dedicated servants of God who were trying, with the information that they had available, to choose wisely, to live righteously, and to preach God's Word as best they could. However, Mormons also feel that all of the churches led by these great men had been established during the time that the Priesthood had been taken off the earth by God (Mormons call it the period of apostasy); and that therefore, these leaders were doing the best they could, in the absence of a prophet of God, who could direct the restoration of the Gospel of Jesus Christ.

Interestingly enough, the Mormon Church grows by about three hundred thousand people a year, just in new births; but it also grows substantially through converts to the Church. And the bulk of those converts are members of other faiths who, although happily believing what they have been taught up to now, have gained a personal testimony that the Mormon Church represents the officially organized Church of Jesus Christ. Most feel enlightened that they've supplemented their prior beliefs with the additional doctrines and principles as taught by The Church of Jesus Christ of Latter-day Saints.

As you meet Mormons around the world, you'll find that many are former Catholics and former Lutherans and former Jews and former Methodists and former Muslims, who have read the Book of Mormon and have prayed for counsel, have felt that they have received such an answer to their prayers and have decided to be baptized and join the Mormon Church.

Q *The Bible is filled with stories about angels and miracles. Why do most churches claim that there are no angels, or miracles, or prophets anymore?*

Most churches claim that there have been no prophets since Biblical times, and that angels and miracles are a thing of the past. Although many believers claim that miracles can and do still occur, most think that miracles occur privately and quietly to their loved ones, or to their family members or friends (when someone is miraculously cured from an illness, or protected from some injury), but that, in general, there are no miracles performed by prophets—because there are no prophets. And most churches say that the time of angels and miracles and prophets is over.

Mormons are baffled by this attitude. Their view is: "Why would God change the system now, when He has always worked through prophets and angelic visitations and miracles?" They believe that God still performs such miracles; that God restored His Church by calling a prophet (and that, upon the death of each prophet, He has called another prophet); that there are Apostles on earth; that there are miracles performed, and revelations given through the prophet to the benefit of mankind; and that angels visit, and miracles occur every day.

It's interesting that some Christian groups attack Mormons for such beliefs. I guess it's a question of whether the glass is half-empty or half-full.

Q Why is it that Mormons have such an affinity for the Jews?

Mormons have a unique relationship with Jews. Whereas most Christian groups view Judaism as being the religion of the Old Testament, and Christianity as being the religion of the New Testament, and that the relationship between the two was merely that some Jews accepted Jesus as the expected Messiah, while most did not.

Mormons have an entirely different view. Their view—based on teachings in the Book of Mormon and other Church Scripture—is that from the time of Adam, all of God's prophets have been Christians.

While the term *Christian* may not have been in use, Mormons believe that God's plan from the beginning was to send Christ to earth to atone for men's sins, to bring to pass the Resurrection, and to provide a way for humans to repent, be forgiven, and return to heaven, from which they came, and that Christ's Church was the same before he was born and crucified, as it was (and is) after.

From this perspective, Mormons believe that Adam was a prophet and a Christian, that Abraham was a prophet and a Christian, that Moses was a prophet and a Christian (while still being a Jew), and so on. When Abraham begat Isaac, and Isaac begat Jacob, and Jacob (who was the one who had his name changed to Israel) begat twelve sons, who became the Twelve Tribes of Israel, Mormons believe that they all were "Christians," because they all taught about the coming of Christ. This is certainly a different approach from what most Christians now believe.

From the Mormon perspective, the Jews—being members of Judah, one of the twelve tribes of Israel—were always Christians. Mormons believe that because the people were unable (or not yet ready) to live the higher laws of Christ, that God instructed Moses to introduce the more structured, preparatory, Law of Moses. But over time, as Mormons see it, the Jews of that time became more focused on the Law of Moses and its strict regulations, than on what the Law of Moses pointed to—the impending arrival of Jesus Christ, the long-awaited Messiah. Jesus Himself said that He had done away with the Law of Moses and the law of sacrifice, because His sacrifice on the Cross was the last sacrifice that Heavenly Father would accept under the Law of Moses.

Mormons believe that they are members of the tribe of Joseph—in the same way that the Jews are members of the tribe of Judah—and that both groups are members of the House of Israel, and both are heirs to the great Abrahamic Covenant. In fact, it is fascinating to learn that, as early as 1845, members of the Mormon faith traveled to Jerusalem in the land of Palestine, one hundred years before Israel was established as a nation, and dedicated the land for the spreading of the Gospel of Jesus Christ.

WHAT KIND OF PEOPLE BECOME MORMONS?

Q   *Why do people join certain churches, and why*
    would anyone want to join the Mormon Church?

Most people join a church either because their parents were
raised in that church, or because they've moved into a new
community and are looking for a church to belong to. And
if they have a religious heritage that's Presbyterian, or Methodist, or Congregationalist, or Jewish, or Catholic, or Mus-
lim, or Lutheran, or Baptist, they'll look for the local place
of worship that is affiliated with that denomination or religion.

For some people, those churches are interchangeable;
they're just looking for a nice church to attend each Sunday,
to have fellowship with other families, and to make friendships with their neighbors in the local community. In that
regard, many people visit a few churches and decide which
to attend, based on who else is there, or if they like the
minister, or if the sermons are good (or short), or if they
would like to join the choir, or what time of day the Sunday
services are held, and so on, and that's the basis of their
decision. Those approaches are not true for Mormons.

People join the Mormon Church because they gain a testimony that the Joseph Smith story is not made up, but is actually true. And therefore, they believe that The Church of Jesus Christ of Latter-day Saints is God's true Church and the same Church that the Savior established when He was on the earth. They believe that Jesus Himself restored this Church through Joseph Smith the prophet, and that the Mormon Church is the only true Church on earth today.

People who do not believe the Joseph Smith story would certainly not join the Mormon Church. People who believe that all churches have a certain element of truth in them, and that God doesn't care which church they belong to, as long as they try to be good Christians, would probably not join the Mormon Church—for the Mormon Church has a much more comprehensive and defined set of doctrines than do most Christian denominations.

Many non-Mormons think that there are way too many doctrines to follow in the Mormon Church. Mormons, on the other hand, haven't chosen their church based on their approval of the doctrines, but rather on their belief that it is God's Church, and therefore they will obey whatever doctrines God has established. Mormons don't see it as difficult to be a Mormon, while non-Mormons sometimes see Mormonism as having lots of requirements and stipulations and time commitments.

It certainly is possible to attend Mormon Church services and never choose to join the Mormon Church. However, most people who feel that they've gained a testimony and have faith that Joseph Smith was telling the truth (and that, indeed, the Mormon Church is God's true Church), do decide to be baptized into the Mormon Church. And once they are members, wherever they live in the world, there is a local congregation of Mormons to attend. And so, for Mormons, it's never a question of *which* local church to attend. Every geographic area in the world is part of some local congregation, and there is no overlap between congregations. Therefore, when a Mormon family moves into a new community, they merely look up where the local Mormon Church is, and that's the church they attend.

Q   *What kind of people join the Mormon Church?*

The Mormon Church is truly an ecumenical religion in that it has former members of nearly every faith on earth among its members. Young people join, old people join, single people join, married people join, Blacks join, Hispanics join, Asians join, Europeans join.

There is no way to categorize the kind of people who join the Mormon Church, except that it is a church made up of people who have made a conscious decision not just to attend a certain church on a corner because it has a good minister, or a pretty building, or because their choir is the most wonderful, but rather because they have been converted to the doctrines of Jesus Christ as taught by The Church of Jesus Christ of Latter-day Saints, and believe that uniting themselves with that church is the right decision for them.

Q Are most Mormons just relatives of those who went to Utah back in the pioneer wagon-train days?

While there are many Mormons who are proud of their ancestral connections to those early pioneers—who struggled and suffered, and had mothers and fathers and brothers and sisters die during those harsh times—most Mormons today are converts to the Church. And therefore, they are the modern-day pioneers who took the courageous and often difficult step to join a church when family ties and long-term family traditions might sometimes be at risk through a decision to become a member of The Church of Jesus Christ of Latter-day Saints.

And although, in any Mormon congregation, perhaps half are converts themselves, and another half are children of parents who were already members of the Church, more often than not, those parents were converts or children of other converts. The Mormon Church is clearly constantly renewed by groups of individuals who are taught the principles of the Gospel, and decide to join the Mormon Church on their own.

This is why the Mormon Church is one of the fastest-growing churches in the world. In contrast to many churches and denominations that are now shrinking, the Mormon Church is growing significantly, and is currently doubling its worldwide membership every ten years or so.

Q Don't Mormons wear old-fashioned black clothes and beards?

For those who don't know any Mormons, or confuse them with other historical American religions such as the Amish, the Mennonites, the Shakers, or the Quakers, it's natural for some people to think that Mormons are rural and old-fashioned and wear period clothing.

The fact is that, aside from all being Christian, there is no connection between those other religions and Mormonism. Mormons are a totally unique American group that was founded in the 1820s and '30s, and has grown from its original six members (the number required by New York State law to establish a church), to more than 11 million members in the year 2001. And although there are many rural members of the Church, especially throughout Utah, Idaho, and California (and in 160 countries throughout the world), Mormons are very much mainstream people who come from all walks of life. There are as many urban and suburban Mormons as there are rural. Wherever there are population centers, a proportion of those people are likely to be members of The Church of Jesus Christ of Latter-day Saints.

Q

Are there any famous people whom I might have heard of who are Mormons?

As of 2001, there are five Mormon senators and eleven Mormon members of Congress. There are governors and judges, and noted physicists and successful businessmen. There are renowned physicians and world-famous inventors. There are best-selling authors (like Steven R. Covey) and TV personalities (like Mike Farrell and Jane Clayson), and film animators (like Don Bluth) and Mothers-of-the-Year and other pageant winners (like Sharlene Wells Hawkes, who was a recent Miss America).

In the sports world, there are football players (like Steve Young, Ty Detmer, and Jason Buck), baseball players (like Dale Murphy), basketball players (like Danny Ainge), Olympic Gold Medal winners (like Peter Vidmar and Rulon Gardner), and golfers (like Johnny Miller, Mike Reid, and Billy Casper).

There are famous entertainers like Donnie and Marie Osmond and the King Family; but few people realize that Gladys Knight (of Gladys Knight and the Pips) was baptized a Mormon in 1997. There are many astronauts and military officers who are Mormon, along with many others who are in the CIA and FBI. The inventor of television—Philo T. Farnsworth—was a Mormon, and, of course, the founders of the Marriott Hotel chain are Mormon (check your hotel room drawer, and you'll find a copy of the Book of Mormon right next to the Gideon's Bible). The fact is that Mormons can be found in nearly all cross-sections of life, in all corners of the globe.

Q Are Mormons pious and self-righteous? Are there any normal people who are Mormons?

You'll have to make this judgment yourself, based on the Mormons that you've met in your own neighborhood, in your own community, and in your own workplace. But in general, Mormons do not see themselves as particularly righteous, or puffed up, or holier than thou. Rather, Mormons believe that they're trying their best to become as Christ-like as they can, but that they have failures and trials, tribulations and weaknesses, and need to repent daily, as do most people.

Most of the time, therefore, you'll find that most Mormons are very normal. They participate in the normal activities of all other community members. They go to work, they try to raise a good family, they have difficulty paying their bills, they try to go to church regularly, they watch TV, they participate in social organizations, they go to school, they play sports, they exercise, they are—in every way—normal residents of the community, with the additional perspective of believing that they're here on earth not just to earn a living and to raise a family, but to also gain eternal happiness by trying to become as Christ-like as they can, and to take advantage of the grace and the opportunities that Jesus has presented to them.

For those who know a lot of Mormons, or live in communities where there are large Mormon populations, they realize that Mormons lead a very *Leave-It-to-Beaver, Father-Knows-Best, Ozzie-and-Harriet* kind of existence. And for those who feel that no one actually lived like the families in those TV sitcoms, they must not know many Mormons, because that's the norm among most Mormon families.

Q *Aren't Mormons racists and anti Blacks?*

Mormons believe in the priesthood of God, and have doctrinal requirements for membership in the priesthood. Up until 1978, Blacks were denied access to the priesthood. They were baptized and encouraged to join the Church, but they were not permitted to hold the priesthood. In 1978, the then current prophet of the Church, Spencer W. Kimball, claimed to have received a revelation from God that it was time to withdraw that obstacle from Black members of the Church, and permit all worthy males the right to be given the Holy Priesthood. As you would imagine, Black membership in the Mormon Church has risen dramatically since that day.

The Mormon Church is not racist (just ask any Black members), but, as with all communities of people, there are always a few who may hold prejudiced views toward certain ethnic groups, contrary to Church teachings. However, the reality is that the Mormon Church has missionaries—including Black missionaries—throughout Africa, throughout South America, throughout Asia, and is baptizing Blacks, and many other ethnic groups, in large numbers. The Church has bishops and other church leaders who are Black, has a growing population (both in the U.S. and abroad) of Black members, and is energized by this new infusion of strong members who believe in the principles of salvation, as taught by Jesus Christ.

Q
Is it true that there are a lot of Mormons in the CIA and the FBI?

Curiously enough, it does appear that there are a lot of members of The Church of Jesus Christ of Latter-day Saints in important security and law enforcement positions. It appears that over many years, the leaders of those organizations have found that there is a distinct need for people who are patriotic, loyal, honest, and serious about their commitments to honor their word, to be involved in law enforcement matters that require top security clearances.

Surprisingly, members of the Mormon faith seem to have those qualifications in higher numbers than their general proportion in the population. Furthermore, while such government agencies are actively looking for people with those qualifications, many Mormons—with a strong set of religious values, and an equally committed love of country—are also looking for such opportunities to serve.

For many years now, America and other countries, have benefited from having honorable Mormons serving in important positions of trust in the FBI, the CIA, and other security agencies, because they are often more loyal and honest, and less likely to succumb to the temptations that might interfere with their job, such as alcohol abuse, gambling, sexual promiscuity, blackmail, and other such activities.

Q Should non-Mormons be wary of making friends with Mormons?

Only if you're worried about hearing some really corny jokes.

Because most Mormons don't drink, swear, smoke, or flirt, their clean-cut image is often tarnished by what seems like a pretty boring lifestyle. But don't be fooled. Mormons are generally a pretty outgoing people, sponsoring neighborhood barbeques, helping with the car pool, volunteering at school, keeping their lawns mowed, and not playing their music too loud. Ask around. You might find that some of your own friends say that some of *their* best friends are Mormon.

Q *Aren't Mormons always just trying to convert their non-Mormon friends?*

It would be hard to give a resounding "No" to this question, because the truth is that Mormons are so enamored with their own faith that they'd like others to be as happy as they are. So, yes, they do try to introduce their non-Mormon friends to their Church.

But Mormons also realize that whether or not a non-Mormon friend is interested in learning more (or even in joining the Mormon Church), is not the measure of the friendship. They'd like to see it happen, but they know that it's a personal decision, driven by true faith and belief, and that everyone has the complete freedom to choose for himself or herself. As with most people, Mormons have close friendships with people of all faiths, and usually try to be good friends themselves.

Q

How can anyone know which church to join? Or if God really exists?

These are certainly some of the more profound questions that have plagued mankind through its entire existence. And as we enter the twenty-first century, there still seem to be as many people as ever who wonder if there is a God, and are confused and baffled by how to determine which church to join.

For many people, determining whether there is a God or not, is mostly based on what they're taught in their youth, with many people merely following in the footsteps of their parents, and others following the claims of ministers, friends, or their own conscience. Believers often respond with the reasons why they know that God exists, and nonbelievers with the reasons why they know God doesn't exist. It usually boils down to a question of personal belief; and, for most people, it's inarguable from either position.

In terms of joining a church, many people, when they move into a new area, visit several churches in the area and select one based on a variety of reasons: how close it is to home, whether the minister gives good sermons, whether it's the prestigious church that you need to be a member of in order to rub shoulders with other movers and shakers in the community; and certainly, for many, it has to do with which denomination or set of doctrines and beliefs each church has.

In the case of Mormons, it's interesting that they claim that there *is* a way for each individual person to determine the answer to the question of which church to join—that method is by reading their Book of Mormon, and then responding to one of the encouragements at the end of that book, which says that if someone were to read this book and pray to God, in the name of Jesus Christ, to find out whether or not the Book of Mormon is true (and represents God's own position), that God will personally answer that person with spiritual confirmation that it is true.

In the eyes of Mormons, this approach enables every person to determine the truthfulness or falsehood of the Book of Mormon for himself or herself, and not to rely on parents, friends, neighbors, missionaries, or others.

And in terms of the question of whether or not God exists, Mormons suggest that the same prayerful method be used. But because many people don't feel that they have the faith necessary to initiate such a prayer, Mormons keep the door open with the following assertion. If *"faith is the substance of things hoped for, the evidence of things not seen,"* (Hebrews 11:1), then hope, alone, can be the starting point for building faith. They assert that if individuals can plant even a tiny seed of hope (that they "desire to believe" the things they're reading), that may be a sufficient expression of faith for God to answer their prayers, and to communicate spiritually with them to confirm that, indeed, He lives, that Jesus Christ is His only begotten Son, and that the Book of Mormon is true.

Q Do Mormons ever participate in Bible study groups?

Sure. But Mormons are typically pretty confident in their understanding of the Bible (they use the *King James Version* exclusively), and often refer to other Mormon Scripture for clarification of certain passages. While this may be stimulating and enlightening to many in the group, it may also prove frustrating to those who don't have access to such Scriptures, or who don't accept such sources as valid. Keep in mind that Mormons would usually be unwelcome if fundamentalists, evangelicals, or anti-Mormons were also in the group.

Mormons also have Scripture study groups of their own, to which non-Mormons are usually welcome to attend.

Q *If Mormons are elected to public office, are they secretly required to obey what their church tells them to do?*

This is the same question that people had when John F. Kennedy ran for president as a Catholic, and when Joseph Lieberman ran for vice president as a Jew. And the answer is the same. No, Mormons are not secretly (or in any other way) told what to do by their church. There are many Mormons in elected public office, both in America and around the world, and they serve with honor, dedication, and a desire to serve the people whom they were elected to represent.

5 POLYGAMY AND OTHER CURIOUS FACTS ABOUT MORMONISM

Q *Most jokes about Mormons have to do with polygamy. What's that about?*

It is true that between the 1850s and 1880s, there was a small number of men in the Mormon Church in Utah who professed to have been "called" by God to have more than one wife. Generally, these men did not want to have more than one wife, but they felt that they were instructed to do so by a prophet of God, as were Abraham and others in the Old Testament.

Because Utah was being considered for statehood, this became a very contentious issue since the law of the United States was that husbands could only have one wife. Wilford Woodruff, who was the Mormon prophet at the time, prayed for inspiration, and asserted that he had been told by God that it was time to end the practice of polygamy, which, even then, was only practiced by fewer than 2 to 3 percent of all the households in Utah.

In obedience to this revelation from God, the practice of polygamy was ended by the Church in 1890. The state of Utah was subsequently admitted to the Union in 1896.

Any Mormons who have been found to practice polygamy since that time have been excommunicated from the Church. For more than 110 years now, Mormons have not practiced polygamy, as it is against the law of the land and in violation of the Law of God. It is, however, an easy target for derision among anti-Mormons, and a common source of Mormon-related "humor" for the rest.

Although there continue to be reports of polygamists who live in Utah and elsewhere, they are not members of the Mormon Church. They might be members of splinter groups who have started their own religions, but they are not members of The Church of Jesus Christ of Latter-day Saints.

Q

What do Mormons have to do with Native American Indians?

This is one of the most fascinating parts of Mormonism, and one of which most non-Mormons are totally unaware.

Most people don't realize that the core historical context of the Book of Mormon is that an Israelite prophet named Lehi, who lived in Jerusalem around 600 B.C., was led by God to flee into the wilderness with his family, in anticipation of the Babylonians taking over and carrying off all of the Jews into slavery. After several years in the wilderness, Lehi and his family were instructed to build a ship and to sail across the ocean, taking with them copies of the first five Books of Moses, and other Old Testament Scriptures, including Isaiah.

The Book of Mormon records that this group of Israelites sailed to the western hemisphere and landed somewhere in Central America.

After Lehi died, two of his sons became leaders of two separate nations. Much of the Book of Mormon records the history of the wars and reconciliations between the remnants of these two powerful groups. Through many stories similar to those recounted in the Old Testament, these two groups fought each other for more than a thousand years, and ultimately became the ancestors of many of the Native American Indians.

And, although it is possible that other peoples came to inhabit the western hemisphere—most scholars think that Asians came over the frozen Bering Strait from Russia and Siberia down through Alaska, and that other Pacific Islanders may have come over on reed boats—Mormons certainly believe that at least one of the groups that inhabited the western hemisphere were remnants of the Jews from Jerusalem, who were led by God to the promised land of the Americas, and who became one of the ancestral groups of the American Indian. And, for this reason, Joseph Smith and the early members of the Mormon Church took the Gospel of Jesus Christ to the various Native American tribes, with considerable success. And even today, there are many Native Americans who are Mormons, and are proud of the fact that, in their eyes, their ancestors were a part of the restoration of Christ's true Church.

Q I've heard of BYU. Is it like other church-affiliated colleges?

The Mormon Church has several different colleges. Brigham Young University (BYU), located in Provo, Utah (about fifty miles south of Salt Lake City), is the oldest and largest, and, in fact, has more than thirty thousand students, making it one of the largest private universities in the world. It offers many undergraduate Bachelor's degree programs, an impressive array of Master's degree programs, doctorate degrees (Ph.D.s), and it even has a law school.

Brigham Young University is about one hundred years old, is funded primarily by the tithing funds of the Church, and therefore is quite inexpensive for both Mormons and non-Mormons. (Although non-Mormons pay roughly a 50 percent tuition surcharge, even that amount is typically less than the in-state tuition charged by most state universities.)

Because of its size, BYU is perhaps the largest university community in the U.S. that is alcohol free. And because 98 percent of the students are Mormons, there is very little drinking, smoking, swearing, or sexual promiscuity, and therefore it is one of the most clean-cut campuses in the world.

BYU is a fully accredited university and is highly regarded for its academic programs. It is somewhat similar to Baylor University for Baptists, and the University of Notre Dame for Catholics, although, at BYU, students are required to sign an agreement saying that they will live by Mormon standards while enrolled as a student. Those behaviors are typically not required at most of the major denominational schools in the U.S., although some of the smaller evangelical Christian colleges do have similar agreements that their students are required to abide by.

The Mormon Church has several other colleges and universities as well, including BYU-Hawaii, BYU-Idaho (formerly named Ricks College), and LDS Business College (in Salt Lake City).

ALL ABOUT MORMON MISSIONARIES

Q *How can you tell the difference between Mormon Missionaries and Jehovah's Witnesses?*

The best way to tell the difference is to ask them. Jehovah's Witnesses are generally hostile toward Mormons, and will be quick to explain that they are certainly *not* Mormon missionaries.

Mormons, on the other hand, tend to be more naïve, and really don't know much about Jehovah's Witnesses.

Mormon missionaries are always seen in twos, either two young men or two young women, or sometimes a retirement-age husband-and-wife couple. They are always modestly dressed, with the men wearing white shirts and ties, and the women wearing dresses (or a skirt and blouse), and they always wear a little black badge that indicates their name and their affiliation with The Church of Jesus Christ of Latter-day Saints.

There are currently more Mormon missionaries than there are missionaries of all other denominations combined. As of 2001, there are more than sixty thousand Mormon missionaries around the world, serving in more than one hundred sixty different countries. Mormon missionaries are usually sent far away from their local home area, and none of them are paid for their service. In fact, all Mormon missionaries pay their own way to go on their missions. Typically, young men go on their two-year mission when they're nineteen years old; and young women go when they're twenty-one.

Q *Why are they usually walking or riding bikes?*

It's already quite expensive for young men and women to save up enough money to go on their missions, without the added cost of purchasing cars, gas, insurance, and parking fees. Although some missions provide cars for missionaries in certain districts for a variety of reasons, most Mormon missionaries either walk or ride bikes.

In urban areas, cars are of little value, when there are forty-floor apartment buildings, with twenty or more apartments on each floor. And in many parts of the world, cars, and even bicycles, are frequently stolen, making walking the common-sense choice for getting around.

Q *How much do Mormon missionaries get paid?*

Mormon missionaries don't get paid anything. They have to pay their own way to go on a mission, and the cost of being sent on a mission was about $400 a month in 2001. As you can see, most missionaries (from the U.S. and Canada) have to save about $10,000 to go on a two-year mission. During their missions, they serve twenty-four hours a day, seven days a week. They're not allowed to hold down jobs, go out on dates, go to the movies, listen to the radio, or watch TV, because they see themselves as full-time servants of the Lord Jesus Christ.

While the Mormon Church hopes that all of its young men decide to go on missions, the truth is that the young men themselves need to apply to go on a mission. And even then, Church leaders may turn them down because of past sins (that may not have been sufficiently repented of, or otherwise might make them temporarily unworthy to serve as missionaries for Jesus Christ); or because of a lack of spiritual commitment; or for other reasons.

Because saving $10,000 is often difficult for a teenager (especially if he or she is from a Third World country or other low-income area), the missionary's parents and extended family frequently help pay that amount, to cover the costs of lodging, food, and transportation. Furthermore, the family's local congregation often pitches in to help send their young men out into the mission field.

Where missionaries are sent is determined by the Church leadership in Salt Lake City. There, Church leaders read over each approved application, and attempt to prayerfully assign each prospective missionary to any one of the Church's nearly three hundred missions around the world.

Each mission is administered by a mission president and his wife (who are also unpaid volunteer missionaries), who watch over, supervise, encourage, protect, and otherwise meet the temporal and spiritual needs of the one hundred sixty to two hundred missionaries in each mission.

A month or two after prospective missionaries submit their application papers, they receive an official letter from Church headquarters indicating where they have been "called" to serve as a full-time missionary for about two years, and when and where they should report for a month or so of training, and up to three months of intensive language skills training, if they've been called to a mission in a country that speaks a language different from the one they speak at home.

Q *Most churches send missionaries to Africa and Asia. Why do Mormons send their missionaries to America and to other places where other churches and religions are already strong?*

Mormons believe that God wants all of His children to return home safely (Mormons believe that all people originally lived in heaven before they were born; they call it the *premortal existence*), to live with Him in heaven, forever, after their time on earth is over. They also believe that they have a duty to spread the Gospel of Jesus Christ to "every nation, kindred, tongue, and people."

From this perspective, Mormons believe that everyone is equal in the sight of God, and that, to be just, all should have the opportunity to hear the Gospel, benefit from the mercy that God extends to all of His children through the Atonement, sacrifice, and Resurrection of Jesus Christ, and to have the freedom to choose to join The Church of Jesus Christ, or not.

To Mormons, it's not a question of "Who are the people most in need of salvation?" but rather, "Who would God want left out?" The answer that Mormons give, of course, is "No one!" They assume that a loving and just Heavenly Father would want *all* of His children to be saved.

And as an aside, those nations (such as the United States) that have incredible affluence and a high standard of living, are also often the same nations that have high levels of immorality and depravity. "Are such people not also in need of salvation?" say the Mormons.

Q *Do Mormons have secret beliefs that are different from what their missionaries teach?*

No. Mormons do not teach one thing and believe another; nor are they trying to "trick" people into joining their church.

The fact is that Mormons are very "regular" people— often not very sophisticated or fancy, just plain people who work hard, try to keep their families together, pray often, go to church regularly, volunteer at school, are friendly and helpful neighbors—who generally are not the kind of people who would try to con someone into joining their church.

To many, Mormons seem to take their religion much more seriously than most people do. And that may be one of the main reasons that some people shy away from joining the Mormon Church—but also why so many people join it. Mormonism is not a go to church twice-a-year, but don't live the principles faith. It provides a framework of understanding that helps to explain every aspect of life on earth. And to many, that framework seems to provide a wonderful reason for living, and a powerful reason for trying to live righteously. To others, the notion that there's a single heavenly plan for all people, simply doesn't fit their worldview.

Q What's the best way to tell Mormon missionaries that you're not interested?

Think about it for a moment. Out of every hundred doors that Mormon missionaries knock on, how many people do you think open their door with a smile, and invite them in to present their message? You're right, not many.

So you can be sure that they're experts in knowing how many different ways people let them know that they're not interested. Never answering the door. Slamming the door in their faces. Swearing at them. Giving some quick-thinking excuse as to why they don't have time to talk.

But all of these responses are pretty harsh and rude, especially when you realize that these are just kids trying to do what they think they're supposed to. Think of it this way: many kids of this age are doing drugs, playing their car radios way too loud, vandalizing your neighborhood, and otherwise behaving poorly. But these guys are wearing suits and ties, not drinking or smoking, not even watching TV, and are talking to people about behaving nicely.

So if you're not interested in listening to them, just say so. But there's no reason not to be pleasant. Remember, they're not getting paid, and are doing their own cooking, so you might want to offer them a cookie or a peanut-butter sandwich. And if you needed to have your lawn mowed, or a room repainted, you might even be able to talk them into helping you out.

And be sure to ask where they're from, because you'll be surprised to find out that, in addition to the ones who come from California, Utah, and Idaho, you're just as apt to find ones who come from Russia, New Zealand, the Czech Republic, Brazil, Uganda, Bulgaria, England, or any of more than a hundred other countries.

Q *Do people who are willing to listen to the Mormon missionaries have any obligation to follow through? Or are they ostracized if they decide not to join the Mormon Church?*

People who listen to what Mormon missionaries have to say, or who invite them into their homes to hear their message, are under no obligation to meet with them again, or to join their church. There is no quota, no "sales" commission for every convert they recruit, and no ill will should someone decide that they're not interested.

The missionaries, of course, would rather answer people's questions, or talk with them about the Gospel of Jesus Christ, than to knock on doors all day, but for roughly two years, this is what they're committed to do, based on their belief that Jesus Christ Himself (through His prophet), has called them to this service.

And they're not doing it for pay, because they don't get paid (in fact, many are delaying college or sacrificing professional sports opportunities), and they're not doing it because they're forced to (as they've all applied voluntarily)— they're doing it out of love, because, in their view, all people on earth are literally brothers and sisters (as children of God), and, like lost sheep, need to be found and given the opportunity to hear about Jesus Christ and His plan for their salvation, and His road map for guiding them back home to heaven.

Q How does someone join the Mormon Church?

Most Christians belong to a local church that is led by a paid minister or pastor. Many of these local churches are affiliated with a larger religious denomination (such as Catholic, Methodist, Baptist, Presbyterian, Lutheran, Episcopal, etc.), but many are not. Membership in these churches is often very informal, and defined solely by where someone attends regularly.

Mormonism has a much more formal and highly organized structure. Each local congregation is a branch that connects directly to the worldwide Church, and being baptized by a priest in the Mormon Church is the only way to become a member.

The official words used by Mormons to baptize someone are as follows:

"Having been commissioned of Jesus Christ, I baptize you in the name of the Father, and of the Son, and of the Holy Ghost. Amen."

—Doctrine & Covenants 20:73

Q Can Mormon missionaries baptize children or teenagers without their parents' permission?

No. To Mormons, the nuclear family unit is God's own plan for how children should be brought into the world and raised, and so Mormons are particularly respectful of all parents' wishes and responsibilities for their children. If a youngster from eight to seventeen years old expresses interest in joining the Mormon Church (Mormons don't baptize anyone until they've reached the age of eight), but his or her parents object, the missionaries will respect that decision and not baptize the young man or woman, unless they subsequently receive parental consent, or until the son or daughter turns eighteen years old.

7 WHY IS MORMONISM SUCH A LIGHTNING ROD FOR PUBLIC SCRUTINY, CRITICISM, AND HOSTILITY?

Q *What is all this commotion about Mormonism? Why are some people so angry and hostile toward Mormons?*

This is a curious question, because, in general, nobody knows much about Mormonism, and most religions aren't hostile or angry toward Mormons at all.

But there do seem to be some fundamentalist Christian groups (including some Southern Baptists and other evangelical groups) that are quite hostile toward Mormons. They feel that Mormons do not accept Jesus Christ as the Savior in the same way that they do. They feel that Mormons are attempting to hide some evil intent behind a false connection to Christianity, and therefore they are quite concerned that members of their own churches are apt to be led away by the "evil Mormons."

This is quite surprising, however, when one realizes that among *other* groups, Mormons are thought of so highly, and are actually sought after. The FBI and CIA, for instance, often try to hire Mormons, because they've learned by experience that Mormons are often more honest than most other people. Furthermore, Mormons (who don't gamble, themselves), are sought after to work in the gambling casinos of Las Vegas, because they are generally much more trustworthy in handling large sums of money than are some non-Mormons. And because active Mormons don't drink, smoke, take drugs, or commit adultery, there are many, therefore, who go out of their way to hire Mormons, because they feel that it reduces the risk of having problems with employees in terms of shoplifting, corruption, and similar things.

Apparently, some of the reasons that some Christian denominations are hostile toward Mormons have to do with the Mormon view of the Trinity, and the Mormon view that men and women can continue to progress eternally, even after death.

Anti-Mormons are also quite quick to (intentionally?) misinterpret and miscommunicate many of the simple beliefs that Mormons hold, by trying to claim that Mormons believe in the Book of Mormon and not the Holy Bible; that Mormons believe Joseph Smith was someone to worship instead of Jesus Christ; and other such misrepresentations.

Why do we hear about anti-Mormons, but not about anti-Methodists, or anti-Lutherans, or anti-Catholics, or anti–other groups?

This is a great question. From their very beginning, Mormons have been persecuted by many different groups, and have been forced out of their communities.

Much of the early story of the Mormon pioneers is about being run out of town, being tarred and feathered, having their homes burned and their belongings stolen, and having their fathers murdered as they tried to practice their religion. In the face of this intense and often bloody persecution, they wound up moving from New York to Ohio, from Ohio to Missouri, from Missouri to Illinois, and from Illinois to Utah—the most desolate desert area in America—where nobody could possibly mind that they were there.

Mormons have always had detractors, and continue to this day to have certain small groups of people who criticize and attack, and attempt to malign the Mormon faith. And although other minority groups around the world have been sorely persecuted over the years, the Mormons have certainly had more than their share of persecution.

But it is interesting that there seem to be very few anti-Protestant groups, especially against any particular denomination. Atheists often mock all religions. And there are individual Muslims who criticize Christianity, and there are individual Christians who criticize Islam. But it is curious that the Mormons seem to attract a more vocal group of hostility than do most other groups.

As a group, Mormons tend to let this just bounce off their backs. They are one of the fastest-growing churches in the world. Their leaders claim to not have time, or interest, in defending themselves against such attacks; and their own Articles of Faith include this statement:

"We claim the privilege of worshipping Almighty God according to the dictates of our own conscience, and allow all men the same privilege, let them worship how, where, or what they may."
—Article 11

In general, Mormons are held in extremely high regard by members of most other faiths and by most government leaders around the world. Their people are hardworking, they're usually loyal employees, they're typically not on welfare, and they're not a drain on society. In fact, they routinely have strong families, are morally pretty "straight-arrow," don't add to the alcohol, drug-use, and illegitimacy problems, and are generally seen as fine neighbors.

It is interesting that the strongest anti-Mormon groups are small, but vocal, and tend to be made up of evangelical Christian groups, for whom there are paid ministers who just might be nervous about losing members of their flock to the Mormon faith. In the case of Mormons, none of the clergy are paid, and therefore there is no monetary benefit to having a large congregation as opposed to a small congregation. In most of these anti-Mormon groups, however, the local ministers are paid directly by the number of people who are members of his or her congregation, and therefore there is a possible incentive to build up the congregation, and to avoid losing membership to another church.

In many churches, the lay leadership discusses how much the minister should get paid, what kind of car they should buy for him or her, and whether or not they should build a parsonage for him or her to live in. (Of course, in some cases, the ministers are allowed to make these decisions for themselves.) However, none of those are issues in a Mormon congregation, because no one gets paid. None of the tithing money goes to the local minister. The local minister (Mormons actually call each local congregation's minister or pastor a *bishop*) has to have a job just like everyone else. And whether or not he can afford a big car or a small car is independent of his participation in his church activities. And therefore a Mormon bishop is just as likely to be a farmer or a building contractor as he is to be the local surgeon or the head of a successful law firm.

Q *Why do some churches call Mormonism a cult?*

There are a few evangelical Christian denominations that feel that Mormonism is a non-Christian cult or sect, out to destroy the faith of their members. Some of these churches actively attempt to thwart Mormonism's success by teaching their own members that Mormons do *not* believe in Jesus Christ, and that Mormons are an anti-Christian group. Although small in number, there are a few such vocal groups that are openly anti-Mormon.

These people, of course, have a right to their own interpretation and beliefs. However, most cults are small groups of followers of one charismatic leader, such as the Jim Jones cult (who followed him to Guyana and committed mass suicide), and the Branch Davidians, who followed David Koresh in Waco, Texas.

To consider Mormonism a cult would be extraordinary, because with more than 11 million members in more than one hundred sixty countries worldwide, worshipping in more than twelve thousand local church buildings, Mormonism is a highly organized worldwide church, that is one of the ten largest Christian denominations in the world.

Mormonism is a large international church. Its members include many millions of devout Christians who believe that theirs is Jesus Christ's own Church. To most people, Mormonism is certainly not a cult but an active and vibrant worldwide Christian church that is highly respected and admired around the world.

Q *Do Mormons attack other churches the way some of them attack the Mormon Church?*

No, the Mormon Church is really quite positive, friendly, and supportive toward all other faiths; and most other faiths are positive, friendly, and supportive toward the Mormons. There are some evangelical Christian denominations that teach that Mormonism is a cult and should be avoided, but there are many that don't teach such things. And while there may be some individual Mormons who are defensive and perhaps not as loving and understanding toward other faiths as they're taught to be, in general, Mormons are grateful that other people and their families are also trying to live Christ-like lives, and are supportive of that. They just wish that other faiths would be equally supportive of their attempts to live Christ-like lives.

The often-unknown reality is that most Mormons are pretty mainstream family members. They go to work, they go to church, their kids play Little League baseball, they go to the public schools, they participate in the PTA, they watch TV, they eat meals together, they say grace, they read the Bible, they engage in the activities that most people in all societies engage in. They just have the added impetus of trying to be righteous and kind, loving and uncritical, and avoid iniquity.

Q Some churches refer to Mormonism as the Anti-christ. Do Mormons believe in the Antichrist? And who do they think it is?

It's true that, as a part of their propaganda, some anti-Mormons preach that Mormonism just might be the Antichrist. However, as Matthew teaches in the New Testament: *"By their fruits ye shall know them."* (Matthew 7:20, but read verses 1–29 for context).

And the *fruits* of Mormonism are really quite remarkable: strong families; moral behavior; honesty; marital fidelity; no drinking, swearing, or smoking; community supporters at every level; the kind of neighbors most people would love to have, people who claim a belief in Jesus Christ and attempt to live their lives as Jesus teaches them to live it—to love their neighbors, to forgive those who have wronged them, to try to be Christ-like in every way.

This does not seem to be the typical behavior of how an Antichrist would behave. Wouldn't an Antichrist be a Hitler type of person? Someone who would teach against Jesus Christ? Someone who would teach against being kind and gentle, loving and charitable?

Mormons don't teach against any of those things. In fact, they embrace those teachings on kindness, love, and charity. They would say that the Antichrists are those wicked world leaders, entertainment moguls, drug kingpins, pornography distributors, etc. who are out to destroy morality, honesty, and righteousness, who are out to destroy happiness, and who are out to destroy families. Mormons merely wonder how it is being Christ-like for one group of Christians to claim that another group of Christians, namely Mormonism, is the Antichrist?

8 WHO WAS JOSEPH SMITH? ALL ABOUT THE FOUNDING OF THE MORMON CHURCH AND ITS PIONEER HERITAGE

Q *Who was Joseph Smith? Do Mormons worship him?*

Joseph Smith was the uneducated son of a farmer, who was born in Vermont in 1805, and moved to New York State with his family in the early 1800s.

By 1820, the little community of Palmyra, New York, was in a period of religious revivalism. In the midst of a series of revival meetings, sponsored by the pastors of several competing churches, fourteen-year-old Joseph Smith was trying to decide which church to join, as were his parents and his brothers and sisters. While reading by candlelight in the New Testament, he came across this passage in the Epistle of James, which said:

> *"If any of you lack wisdom, let him ask of God, that giveth to all men liberally, and upbraideth not; and it shall be given him."*
>
> —James 1:5

According to Mormons, when the young Joseph read this passage, he recognized himself to be someone who "lacked wisdom," so he went out into the woods and knelt down to pray. It was at that point that he asserted that God the Father and Jesus Christ appeared to him. He claimed that they instructed him not to join any of the churches; and, that if he would remain worthy, he would be an instrument in God's hand to reestablish the true Church of Jesus Christ.

Joseph Smith, therefore, is the man that Mormons see as the first prophet in these, the "latter days." He is not, however, someone that they worship or consider to be at the head of their church. They consider Jesus Christ to be the head of their church. Mormons believe that God uses prophets (as they claim He always has) to communicate to His Church, and, in this case, He communicated through His chosen prophet, the young Joseph Smith.

Soon after this first vision, Joseph Smith was led to where the Book of Mormon had been buried, and was instructed as to how to reestablish the Church.

For Mormons, this visit to Joseph Smith by God the Father and His Son, Jesus Christ, was a miraculous event. They see it as a turning point in the history of the world. But for those who believe that this event did not occur, they maintain that this whole story was merely a hoax, dreamt up by Joseph Smith, and other "troublemakers."

Mormons merely say that everyone has the right to believe what they want to, but for them, if God could part the Red Sea, could flood the earth in Noah's time, could lead Jacob's son Joseph (having been abandoned by his brothers in the pit) to become the second most powerful person in Egypt, that if God could perform those miracles, why would He not also choose to select a young fourteen-year-old boy (as He did with young David, to slay Goliath), and have him restore the true Church of Jesus Christ for the benefit of all mankind?

Q *Where did the Mormon Church come from?*

Most non-Mormons are curious about the origination of the Mormon Church, and wonder if it was the idea of someone like Martin Luther for the Lutherans, or John Wesley for the Methodists, or Mary Baker Eddy for the Christian Scientists. Frankly, many assume that this person, Joseph Smith, started the Mormon Church.

Mormons, however, explain the background of the establishment of the Mormon Church quite differently. First, they will probably clarify to the reader that there really is no such thing as the Mormon Church. The official name of the church is The Church of Jesus Christ of Latter-day Saints; and they will go on to say that it was anti-Mormons who mockingly referred to members of this church as Mormons, because they didn't want to acknowledge or admit that these people claimed to be Christians.

Second, Mormons contend that all of God's prophets throughout the history of the world have been members of His Church, called the Church of Jesus Christ. They believe, therefore, that all of the prophets in the Bible were members of the Church of Jesus Christ. Mormons believe that Adam and Eve were members of this church; that Noah and his family were members of this church; that Abraham, Isaac, and Jacob (and the Twelve Tribes of Israel) were all members of this church; that Joseph who was sold into Egypt was a member of this church; that Moses was a member of this church . . . and that all of these early prophets taught of the coming of the Messiah and Savior, the Lord Jesus Christ.

Mormons believe that Jesus Christ has always been the head of God's Church, and that, upon His birth, He merely reaffirmed the key doctrines of the Church that had remained unchanged. Upon His death, and the death of the Apostles, Mormons believe that God took the authority to administer the affairs of the Church from the earth; and they contend that the period between about 100 A.D. and the restoration of their church in 1820, represents a period of apostasy from the true Gospel of Jesus Christ. They assume that that's why everyone calls much of that period the Dark Ages.

Refer to the Index to find out where in this book you can read more about Joseph Smith and his claim to have found the Book of Mormon, but it is the Mormons' contention that Joseph Smith was merely the young boy selected by God the Father to be the instrument for the reestablishment of Christ's original Church on the earth. In that regard, Mormons believe that theirs is the same church that Jesus established, that it is once again available on the earth, and that it is God's Church.

It might be interesting to note that Mormons call their church The Church of Jesus Christ of Latter-day Saints, to differentiate it from the pre-apostasy church, which might now be referred to as The Church of Jesus Christ of *Former-day* Saints.

Q *Is it true that Joseph Smith really claimed to have been visited by God and Jesus, and even angels?*

Yes. And this is one of the key components of the Mormon faith. Nearly all of their belief system is based on their firm contention that this event really occurred.

Q Did anyone else claim to see these visitations or these angels?

Yes, there are other early Mormons (and some subsequent to that time), who claim to have also been in attendance when these heavenly visitations occurred. They even signed legal affidavits to that effect, and none ever rescinded those affidavits, even though several left the Mormon Church.

It is a part of the Mormons' interpretation of God's Plan of Salvation that hard evidence will be withheld from mankind, in order to force men and women to base their belief in the Lord Jesus Christ on faith, rather than on proof. They believe, as they claim the Scriptures have taught over and over again, that those who seek for a sign have been given enough signs, and that "faith precedes the miracle." They would say that any miracles come *after* faith is exercised, and that to look for a miracle in order to *justify* your faith, is to miss the point. Mormons encourage everyone to exercise faith, and pray for confirmation that you're on the right track, and God will provide such confirmation.

In order to further show that Joseph Smith was not alone in his claims, Mormons believe that God allowed certain selected witnesses to also see angels, handle the golden plates, and hear the voice of the Lord, so that there would be more than one witness to the truthfulness of the things Joseph told them. They believe, as the Scriptures state in 2 Corinthians 13:1, that: *"In the mouth of two or three witnesses shall every word be established."* Mormons believe that Joseph Smith was telling the truth, and that God provided several witnesses to reaffirm that contention; and most Mormons will tell you that they've each gained a personal testimony of the truthfulness of these things through spiritual occurrences in their own lives.

For non-Mormons, of course, they must decide for themselves whether Mormonism represents God's true Church. Mormons merely encourage them to sincerely pray about it, having faith in Jesus Christ that He'll reveal the truth to them.

Q *The golden plates that were the basis of the Book of Mormon were supposedly found in a hill in Upstate New York. Were such burials ever used in ancient times? Or found by other archeologists?*

Interestingly enough, there have been archeological discoveries—long after Joseph Smith's death—that are very similar to what was claimed for the Book of Mormon. Joseph Smith claimed that there was a loose-leaf set of flat brass and gold plates, that were connected by metal rings, and that were buried in a stone box that was sealed on all six sides, the top, the bottom, and all four sides.

Similar boxes have been uncovered in other parts of the world, in South America, Persia, and the Middle East. And other ancient writings have also been found, that were organized in similar loose-leaf fashion.

9   ALL ABOUT MORMON CULTURE: HUMOR,
     GENEALOGY, PATRIOTISM, THE MORMON
     TABERNACLE CHOIR, YOUTH PROGRAMS, AND
     SO ON

Q   *Do Mormons have a sense of humor?*

While some might call it a sense of humor, others might
think that it is so cheesy that it can't be qualified as humor.
The fact is that because most Mormons don't swear, engage
in illicit sex, drink alcohol, or tell off-color stories, most
Mormon humor is pretty much from the *Leave It to Beaver*
era. Here are a few examples:

- *Remember when they said that if you played a certain
  Beatles album backward, that you could hear the words:
  "Paul is Dead"? That was a widely spread rumor back
  in the late 1960s. Or that you could hear satanic messages, if you played certain hard-rock albums backward?
  Well, do you know what happens when you play Mormon Tabernacle Choir records backward? You get 139
  different lasagna recipes.*

- *Did you see the article in* The New York Times *that
  mentioned that archeologists have recently uncovered evi-*

dence from Old Testament times about Abraham and his son Isaac? There has always been some question as to how old Isaac was when God commanded Abraham to take him to the top of the mountain and sacrifice him. Well, the article goes on to say that it appears that Isaac must have been either under thirteen, or over nineteen, because if he had been a teenager it couldn't have been considered a sacrifice.

• How many Mormons does it take to change a lightbulb? About 250: Five to arrange the program, ten to set up the chairs, three to decide on the music, one to play the organ, one to conduct the choir, those whose names begin with A–G to bring salads, H–M to bring main dishes, N–Z to bring desserts, one to say the opening prayer, one to say the closing prayer, all of the men to put the chairs away, five to stack the hymnals . . .

• Did you ever wonder why Mormons stop having kids at thirty-nine? Because forty is just too many!!

Q Why do Mormons refer to each other as Brother So-and-So and Sister So-and-So? That seems so old-fashioned.

There certainly aren't many religious denominations or congregations that continue to use this terminology, although many of the Amish-related groups and African-American churches still do, as do some of the evangelical Christian groups.

In Mormonism's case, this is simply a way of reinforcing what Mormons consider to be the eternal relationship that all humans have with each other. Mormons believe that God is the spiritual Father of all the children who have ever been born on the earth. And because of that, all of the people on earth—including members of every single race—are one another's brothers and sisters.

This not only reinforces the sense of relationship among all members of the Church, but it strengthens each local congregation by establishing a greater sense of family among the Church community at the local level. Non-Mormons see this as old-fashioned or quaint; Mormons see it as normal and an endearing part of their faith and heritage.

Q How come when I look up the Mormon Church in the phone book, there are no listings?

Although some local congregations *do* put an additional listing in the white or yellow pages under the name "Mormon Church," the official name of the Church is The Church of Jesus Christ of Latter-day Saints, and that's where most phone books list the Church. And because listings in the yellow pages usually cost money (and local Mormon congregations have very limited budgets), Mormons often don't pay to have a special yellow pages listing.

Typically, Mormon Church phone numbers are listed in the white pages listing, either under the "Church of Jesus Christ" or, if they're grouped by category, under "Churches."

Because Mormons have no paid ministry, the bishop of each local congregation (Mormons call them *wards*), has a job, just like everyone else does, and only serves as the minister in a voluntary capacity. Therefore, there is typically no church office with people answering the phone during normal business hours. The bishop is usually reached at home in the evenings; and on Sundays, of course, there are people in the church offices conducting the meetings that run the local congregation, both before and after Sunday worship services.

Given this reality, it's often somewhat difficult for non-Mormons or visitors to get through to a Mormon Church by phone, except on Sunday mornings. To cover this eventuality, some wards include other listings under the Church's name in the phone book, providing the home phone numbers of the local bishop, the Relief Society president (the women's program leader), the Institute director (the head of the local educational program for college students), or the missionaries; and some have an answering machine that will take messages or provide information about where each local chapel is located, how to get there, when Sunday services are held, and so on.

Q Why are Mormons so interested in tracing their roots and doing genealogy?

Mormons believe that all the people who live on earth are the children of God, who is their Heavenly Father, and that, as children of the same God, they are ultimately all brothers and sisters, and part of the same family.

Genealogy work—or tracing one's ancestors—is all about linking families together.

Mormons have several reasons for getting involved in genealogy work. One reason is that it's fun to learn more about your grandparents, your great-grandparents, and so on, and to learn as much as possible about their lives, what trials they went through, and what was important to them. Mormons try to gather birth, marriage, and death certificates, military service records, old diaries, early photographs, and other memorabilia from their ancestors, and often claim that they develop a renewed appreciation and admiration for these relatives whom they never knew personally.

Another reason Mormons get involved in genealogy work is because they believe that certain religious ordinances—like Baptism—are required of all, but which may not have occurred for many millions of people who lived on the earth but who—through no fault of their own—never had the opportunity of hearing about the Gospel of Jesus Christ, or being baptized in His name.

For these deceased people, Mormons believe that they can baptize them, by proxy, in their sacred temples, so that, should they decide to hear the Gospel in heaven and join the Church, they will have already had the required ordinances performed for them, in the same way that Christ performed a proxy sacrifice—through his Atonement and

Crucifixion—so that everyone may have the opportunity to repent and be cleansed from sin.

To non-Mormons, this is a pretty unusual doctrine. However, Mormons refer the curious to 1 Corinthians 15:29, wherein the Apostle Paul asks:

"Else what shall they do which are baptized for the dead, if the dead rise not at all? Why are they then baptized for the dead?"

Rather than seeing this doctrine as odd, Mormons see it as wonderful, a remarkable indication of both the justice and mercy of a loving God. While most faiths see non-members of their own faith as doomed to some form of hell, Mormons believe that a just God would not permit *some* of his children to be saved, while others are doomed, just because they happened to be born in different circumstances, in different times, and to parents of different faiths.

Mormons believe that it's not just tough luck that the Aborigines never got to hear the Gospel preached, or the Africans, or the early Egyptians, or the Greeks, or the Native Americans, or the millions of people in Asia. Mormons don't think God would deny these people access to Christ's Plan of Salvation. Therefore, Mormons claim that by performing Baptisms and other sacred ordinances for these people who have died, they keep open their opportunities for gaining entrance to heaven. And this is why they're so focused on acquiring the genealogical records of all of the people who have ever lived. (Mormons even claim that, during the Millennium, the information about those people whose records either never existed or have been destroyed will be made available, so that no one is overlooked.)

Q Do Mormons have charitable efforts? Or welfare programs for the poor?

Actually, the Mormon Church has an extensive charitable program that distributes significant amounts of humanitarian supplies and services around the world (to both Mormons and non-Mormons); and it administers an elaborate welfare program for Church members facing hard times.

Because of its presence in more than one hundred sixty countries around the world—coupled with its centralized hierarchy—the Mormon Church is able to respond quickly, and with surprising efficiency, to most major worldwide natural disasters such as earthquakes, volcanic eruptions, floods, landslides, tidal waves, etc., as well as to other crises such as famines, epidemics, war-torn refugees, etc.

Often, it's Mormon Church aid that, in response to global disasters, is among the first on the scene. And the Church often works hand-in-hand with the Red Cross, the Salvation Army, Catholic Social Services, and other prominent international relief organizations to coordinate the delivery of urgently needed food supplies, medical equipment, and manpower.

In terms of welfare programs for the poor, the Mormon Church's welfare system has long been a model for governments and private organizations around the world. It is based on two simple concepts. First, that every husband should provide for his own family's temporal needs such as food, shelter, clothing, education, transportation, medical care, etc. And second, that when circumstances make it difficult or impossible to meet those needs, fellow Church members will be there to help out.

That's a nice thought, in theory, but you might ask: "Does it ever really work in the real world?" And the fact is that the Mormons have found a way to make it work, and here's how they do it.

Once a month, Mormons *fast* (abstain from eating any food, or drinking any water or other drinks) for twenty-four hours, or at least two meals a day. Simultaneously, they donate the amount of money they would have spent for eating and drinking that day to their local congregation as a *fast offering*. Monthly, these combined fast offerings provide the local bishop with a small pool of funds, which he is authorized to disburse (under certain prescribed conditions) to those members of his ward who have emergency needs (often caused by unemployment, illness, accidents, or other emergencies).

What doesn't get used in any given month is then transferred to the stake level (a term Mormons use for diocese, or group of five to ten wards), where it can be used to supplement needs in other wards. And, likewise, what doesn't get used at the stake level, is then transferred to Church headquarters in Salt Lake City, where it can be used to supplement needs in other stakes, anywhere in the world.

In this way, small donations (which cost the donor nothing, because the food that the money would have gone to purchase wasn't eaten) get pooled together to provide funds that can be used to help those in need anywhere in the Church. If surpluses exist, they get passed along; if local needs are greater than the amount of funds in the pool, then such funds can be drawn down from the next level up. It really is a remarkable system.

Other components of the Mormon Church's welfare program include regional employment offices, which both keep track of people in need of work (or in need of upgrading their employment situation), and keep track of available employment opportunities in each region; regional welfare farms and canneries, where the Church can grow and can its own food for distribution where it's needed (while also providing employment opportunities for those receiving Church welfare); and the Church's well-known "year's supply of food" program, through which all Mormon families are encouraged to stock up enough food, medicine, water, and other important supplies, to help sustain them for up to a year, in the event of some natural disaster or long-term unemployment emergency.

Q   *What kind of youth programs does the Mormon Church have, both for teenagers as well as for younger children?*

Here's the breakdown by age group of the youth programs offered to Mormon families.

• *Birth to eighteen months:* This infant and toddler stage is when most children stay with their mothers and are usually held during church services by mother, father, siblings, or others.

• *Eighteen months to three years:* Although these toddlers usually sit with their families during the main hour-long Sacrament meeting worship service, they attend a special nursery for the remaining two hours, providing them with a combination of rest, play, socialization with other toddlers, and simple Gospel training.

• *Age three to twelve years:* For these preteens, the Mormon Church runs what it calls the Primary Organization. This organization is a Sunday School program with classes for each individual age group. Children in these ages attend classes for two hours each Sunday, where they learn principles from the Bible—both the Old and New Testaments—and from the Book of Mormon, and read Scriptures, participate in activities, listen to lessons, engage in skits and class projects, give talks in front of their classmates, learn how to give prayers, and so on. Starting at eight years old, these Primary children also have a twice-a-month after-school activity, which further prepares them for adolescence.

• *Age twelve to eighteen years:* Once Mormon children reach the age of twelve, and continuing through the age of eighteen (which is primarily the sixth through the twelfth grade levels in school), they leave the Primary Organization and go into what Mormons call the Young Men's and Young Women's Organizations. Each Sunday, during the one hour Mormons set aside for adult Sunday School, these youth attend Sunday School classes with other members their age. And during a second hour, they attend classes that are separated by sex, so that all of the teenage girls go into the Young Women's Organization, and all of the teenage boys go into the Young Men's Organization, where they are given additional Gospel training. In addition, all of these teenagers have a once-a-week evening Activity Night, which is often made up of short lessons, skill workshops, scouting activities, service projects, recreational sports and games, and always refreshments.

• *Grades nine through twelve:* Once Mormon youth enter high school, they're also involved in what the Mormon Church calls their Seminary program, which, for most Mormons around the world, is an early-morning Bible study group, that meets for about an hour every day before school. In addition to Seminary, Mormons also have special Super Saturday activities, summer camps for both young men and young women, and annual youth conferences.

As you can tell, the Mormon Church has many programs for youth, and maybe that helps to explain why Mormon youth are often known as being better behaved, more respectful of their elders, more honest, more hardworking, more willing to serve others, and less apt to cause trouble than many other youth groups.

Q Are Mormons allowed to watch TV, listen to the radio, or go to sporting events?

Sure. Mormons are much more mainstream and normal than many people realize. They watch TV, play video and computer games, listen to the radio, have CD collections, and are often sports fanatics. Because most Mormon Church buildings also have an indoor basketball court, many Mormons—both men and women—develop an avid love for the game of basketball. In fact, many Mormon stakes sponsor Church basketball leagues, in which non-Mormon friends are encouraged to participate.

Q Do Mormons believe in singing or dancing?

This may seem like an odd question to many, but there are some religions that do not allow singing or dancing among their members, so, for those people, this is a legitimate question. And the answer, as it pertains to Mormons, is a resounding "yes."

Hymn singing has been an important part of Mormon life from its inception. And, being a Christian religion, the Mormon hymnal has many of the favorite traditional Protestant hymns and Christmas carols in its pages. And of course, the Mormon Tabernacle Choir is perhaps the most famous choir in the world. In fact, the dramatic image of the remarkable organ in the Mormon Tabernacle, in Salt Lake City, is possibly even more recognizable than the six spires of the Salt Lake Temple.

Similarly, Mormons have long felt that dancing was a healthy outlet and social pastime, and sponsor all kinds of dance festivals, youth dances (for those fourteen and up), and square dances. And for those of you into ballroom dancing, you're probably already aware that BYU (Brigham Young University) has won many national ballroom dancing championships over the years.

Q Are Mormon teenagers allowed to listen to rock music of any kind?

Mormons believe in freedom of choice, so of course there are no formal restrictions on members' listening habits. Mormon grandparents listened to big band and swing music back in the 1940s; Mormon parents listened to Elvis, Motown, and the Beatles in the '50s and '60s; and Mormon teenagers now listen to U2, the Dixie Chicks, and Moby. Do their parents always appreciate it? Probably not. But do the kids listen to it? You bet.

Now, that's not to say that Mormon leaders are pleased with all of the music that's being played today. In addition to the many great things that are being written and performed, there are also a lot of songs that use foul language, refer to drugs and sexual behavior, and are just not very uplifting or positive. Mormons are encouraged not to listen to or buy such music.

Q *Is it true that Mormons try not to shop, work, or play sports on Sundays?*

Mormons believe in honoring the Sabbath Day. Their church worship services are held on Sundays, and they try to reserve Sundays for family time, church attendance, serving others, and rest.

Do some Mormons have jobs that require them to work on Sundays? Yes, some do. Do some Mormons play professional sports that require them to play on Sundays? Yes, some do. But, in general, Mormons try to refrain from going to the mall, doing their grocery shopping, buying gas, going to the swimming pool, or going to work on Sundays. They see it as a way to show God that they're serious about trying to keep His commandments, but also as a way to bring the family together, to rest from a long week's worth of work, to regroup, to get refreshed, and to prepare to take on whatever challenges will arise in the week to come. They also like the fact that, by not doing the same things that they do on every other day of the week, it makes Sundays more special, something to look forward to.

Q *Are Mormons allowed to say the Pledge of Allegiance to the flag?*

Mormons in the United States tend to be a very loyal and patriotic group of people. They're grateful for the freedoms that America provides, and are proud to be able to recite the Pledge of Allegiance. In fact, it's interesting to note that one of their basic tenets is to support and uphold the laws of the land. As their Articles of Faith states:

"We believe in being subject to kings, presidents, rulers, and magistrates, in obeying, honoring, and sustaining the law."

—Article 12

Because of this doctrine, Mormons who live in countries all over the world, and under all forms of governments, have established a reputation for themselves as being loyal, law-abiding citizens.

Q *Don't Mormons all think alike? Aren't they all commanded to behave a certain way, and vote a certain way?*

Freedom of choice (Mormons favor the term *free agency*) is an important element of their Church doctrine. They believe that God gives commandments, but that people have the freedom to obey or not to obey.

With this as a starting point, you would expect Mormons to be pretty much in agreement when it comes to Church doctrine and beliefs. And that's so, as people who don't agree with Mormon tenets would probably not choose to join the Mormon Church in the first place. But when you look beyond Church doctrine, you'll quickly find that not all Mormons think alike.

Among the Mormons, there are avid Republicans, and avid Democrats; loyal union members, and those who are anti-union; sincere environmentalists, and ardent nuclear power advocates; fanatic BYU fans, and just as fanatic University of Utah and Utah State fans. In other words, Mormons can be as passionate about politics, sports, and music, as they are about religion. But the divergence of opinions among Mormons on these other issues is apt to be as broad as among the rest of the population.

MORAL STANDARDS AMONG MORMONS

Q *Why don't Mormons go to R-rated movies?*

Most Mormons would respond to this question by asking: "Why would anyone go to an *R-* (or worse) rated movie?"

There are, of course, some Mormons who will occasionally go to an R-rated movie. But in general, Mormons (as Christians who are trying to be good), lament the apparent decline in morality around the world, and—because of their belief in Jesus Christ, and their desire to live life righteously—most are trying to raise their families in a more wholesome environment.

Many people—Catholics, Jews, evangelical Christians, Muslims, and those of many other faiths, including Mormons—are genuinely concerned about the moral vacuum they feel seems to pervade much of Western culture these days. Mormons tend to believe that the entertainment industry—including Hollywood and the TV studios—often depicts inappropriate sexual, drug-related, or other immoral behavior as "normal," and that these depictions send a dangerous message to viewers, especially young people, whose worldview is heavily determined by the images they see on TV and in the movies.

Although the R rating is arbitrary and not always consistent, it is an easy-to-identify dividing line between those movies that have nudity, a greater depiction of immorality, of drinking, of particularly foul language, and of other inappropriate behavior, and Mormons try to limit their exposure to those things (as do members of many other churches).

Q

What's the Mormon attitude toward sex and dating?

With married Mormon and Catholic couples having many more children than the average family in most countries, it's obvious that Mormons have a positive attitude toward sex. The only caveat is that Mormons believe that *all* sexual relations must only occur between husbands and wives who are legally married to each other, and that all other sexual activity is improper, against God's plan for our salvation, and will ultimately lead to unhappiness and tragedy.

Therefore, the Mormon Church teaches its members to avoid all premarital sex, all extramarital sex, all homosexual sex, all telephone sex, all pornography, and all media attempts (mostly TV and movies) to portray such sexual activity as normal and healthy, and without unhappy consequences.

The Mormon refrain is: "No sex outside of marriage, and total fidelity within marriage."

And although not all Mormons live up to these standards (some fall, but then repent, while others just fall, and slip away), the fact that most Mormons do live up to these standards helps to explain their low divorce rates, low HIV/AIDS rates, and high family-togetherness rates.

In terms of dating, Mormons generally permit group dating at the age of sixteen . . . but discourage pairing off until teens are older, in order to avoid temptations related to alcohol, drugs, sex, etc., that nearly always lead to unhappiness . . . and sometimes to heartbreak and tragedy.

Q   *What is the Mormon attitude toward abortion?*

Because Mormons believe that all humans born on the earth have already been existing, in spirit form, with God in heaven, they feel that every child born is a distinct son or daughter of God, who deserves to live a full life and return home to heaven as a resurrected being after this life is over.

Their view is that it's the parents' responsibility to *raise* their children, not *terminate* them. And most Mormons see abortion as merely a quick and easy escape from having to face the consequences of having had sex either outside of marriage, or within a marriage where children are seen as an inconvenient interference, rather than as a blessing.

Of course, in cases of rape or other tragic circumstances, the Mormon Church allows families the freedom to make their own decisions; but, in general, Mormons choose to carry such babies to term, and then put them up for adoption, since there are many families who would love to be able to raise children, but who are unable to have any of their own.

Q Is it true that Mormons try not to use any profanity?

You've heard of hippies being "stuck in the 1960s"? Well, Mormonism is very much "stuck in the 1950s" in a *Leave It to Beaver, Father Knows Best* (but if you remember, it was always *Mother* who knew best), *Mayberry* sort of a world. (Did you ever hear a swear word coming out of Aunt Bea?)

Now, many would laugh at that, and mock the Mormons for longing for a time that can't be brought back, and that many say never really existed anyway.

And sure, every family has its crises, its arguments, and its weird old Uncle So-and-So. But you'd be surprised how pleasant it is to have families that pray together each morning, study the Holy Scriptures briefly each week, go to work, go to school, volunteer in a classroom, do their household chores, sit down together for dinner each night, turn off the TV to do homework, have family councils, plan family vacations, visit local nursing homes, go to church together on Sundays, and still be able to Instant-Message their friends on the computer, play high school football, go out to dinner, and do all of the other things that most families do.

Is profanity needed to make any of this work? Does it improve anyone's communication? Mormons merely wonder why Americans are so willing to let themselves be swayed by the foul language that has become so prevalent on TV, in the movies, and at school. (And, of course, Mormons would certainly never want to take the Lord's name in vain.)

Q *Are Mormons really this good?*

Members of The Church of Jesus Christ of Latter-day Saints are a cross-section of every possible kind of person you can imagine. Are they perfect? Of course not. Are they sinless? Of course not.

But most are sincerely trying to get better, little by little, day by day. They try to be honest. They try to be charitable. They try to be friendly and helpful. They have a great deal of faith, and are trying to find those often elusive ways to align the harsh realities of the real world with what they believe to be the true reasons God put men and women on the earth.

Are they rich? Very few are monetarily rich, but many are spiritually rich. Are they debt free? Many are, but many are not. Are they always loving and kind? Many are, but, like most people, some days go better than others. And what a worker thinks of his forty-year-old boss may be quite different from what the boss' fifteen-year-old son thinks of him sometimes.

So are Mormons really as good as they're often portrayed? Sometimes yes, and sometimes no. Do Mormons think they're better than other people? A few probably do; but the vast majority of Mormons are pretty humble, plain folk who are just trying to make it through each day, and get a little more Christ-like, one day at a time. Like most people everywhere, they're trying to be better; they slip sometimes, but they're grateful to Jesus Christ for providing a way to repent, so that their mistakes can be washed away, and they can give it another try tomorrow.

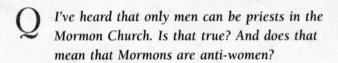

Q   *I've heard that only men can be priests in the Mormon Church. Is that true? And does that mean that Mormons are anti-women?*

Ordaining women to the ministry is certainly a controversial issue in many churches and denominations around the world, including the Catholic Church. For nonbelievers, and members of other churches who do not believe in Mormon doctrines, they see this males-only policy as being one that is unacceptably chauvinistic and anti-women.

For Mormons—including Mormon women—however, this policy is not seen as either chauvinistic or anti-women at all. It is true that only male members (in good standing), are permitted to hold the various levels of priesthood (ordained clergy positions) in the Mormon Church; but to Mormons, this is merely obedience to the direct commandments of God, rather than obedience to a doctrine determined by the preferences of the men in the Church.

The Mormon Church is not a church where the doctrinal principles are voted on by the membership. Doctrine is given through the Scriptures, and by God's prophet and the Twelve Apostles. Each and every member has the full freedom to follow those principles or not, or to choose to join some other church.

In the case of the Mormon Church (if one were to ask), nearly all female members would indicate that they fully support the Church's position on only males being allowed to hold the priesthood; and, in fact, most women would state that they have significant responsibilities in the Church, and that, in many ways, they are the driving force behind their husbands' priesthood service. Women hold positions at all levels within the Church. They are teachers, administrators, leaders, and companions (with their husbands), in family and Church decisions.

In fact, unlike the doctrine in many other religions, Mormons believe that only husbands and wives, *together,* can attain the highest level of eternal life in heaven; and that if either has proven unrighteous, or is unfair or abusive toward their spouse, they will be denied access to that highest degree of heaven. Given this perspective, the partnership between husbands and wives in the Mormon Church is an important and significant eternal bond.

Furthermore (although this is not a widely publicized belief, it's nonetheless true), Mormons believe that there is a *Heavenly Mother* in addition to a Heavenly Father. They believe that if all of the people on earth have been created by God, and that if men were created in the image of God, then of course so were women. Furthermore, Mormons believe that the only way to create children is to have both a father and a mother; and that the family system on earth is merely a microcosm of the eternal family system in heaven.

Given this understanding, it's naïve for people to think of the Mormon Church as being anti-women, when, indeed, Mormons believe that we have heavenly parents, with Heavenly Father married to Heavenly Mother. While some other churches and religions may allow women to become members of the clergy, it's only the Mormon Church (among the major religions) that believes that there is a Heavenly Mother. This and the opportunity to return to heaven on an equal footing—men and women, husbands and wives, still married after death—is unique to the doctrines and beliefs of the Mormon Church.

Q Is there any organization for women in the Mormon Church?

It might come as a surprise to most people, but the largest organization for women on earth is the Mormon Church's Relief Society. It was founded in 1842, in the city of Nauvoo, Illinois (which, at that time, rivaled Chicago as the largest city in Illinois, until the Mormons had to abandon it in 1846).

Now approaching 3 million members worldwide, it has a local chapter in every congregation in the Church, and, under the leadership of local Mormon women, provides friendship and fellowship; teaches the Gospel; conducts workshops on marriage relationships, parenting, careers, home finances, health matters, educational pursuits, cultural enrichment, literacy, homemaking, etc.; organizes service projects; and administers an elaborate system of visiting each other at least once a month.

Each congregation's Relief Society meets weekly, on Sundays, as a part of the three-hour Mormon worship service. It also meets one evening a month for workshops and special activities, and several other times throughout the year, in combined meetings with the five to ten other ward Relief Societies in the same stake (diocese or parish). Attendance at these meetings is open to all, and many Mormon women routinely invite their friends and neighbors to join them at these meetings.

Q What is the Mormon attitude toward mothers and wives working?

All things being equal, Mormons believe that it is the father's primary responsibility to earn a living for the family, and the mother's primary responsibility to raise the children. However, there are many cases where those options are not available, and there are even some families that choose to have the father be the at-home nurturer and the mother out working.

Mormons generally believe, however, that it is a detriment to the children, and to the overall family well-being, for both parents to work—unless absolutely necessary—because they believe children will do better in school, will grow up with a more positive attitude, a healthier work ethic, and stronger morals with an at-home mom than they would otherwise.

Typically, Mormons will believe that the sacrifice of keeping the mother at home and trying to live on a smaller income, is a much preferred choice to having a more affluent lifestyle—with both parents working—but without the benefit of having one of the parents at home to raise the children. And while all Mormon families have the full freedom to make these decisions themselves, the counsel from Mormon Church leaders is that it is preferable for the mother to stay home and raise the children, and for the father to engage in honorable, meaningful work to pay the bills.

12

HEALTH ISSUES

Q Why are Mormon health statistics so much better than most other groups?

One of the revelations that Joseph Smith claimed to have received from Jesus Christ way back in the 1830s was the revelation that the Mormons call *The Word of Wisdom*. This revelation encouraged members of the Church not to smoke, drink alcohol, or consume coffee or tea. All of these were quite common practices in the frontier churches of the day, and are still quite common among all civilizations on the earth.

But because Mormons have not engaged in those practices for many generations now, there is a general healthiness among Mormons that is surprising. The rates of lung cancer are lower, the rates of heart disease are lower, and the rates of other tragedies in terms of family breakups and accidents due to alcoholism are also lower.

In general, Mormons have been taught from childhood on not to smoke or drink alcohol, and to avoid coffee and tea, and this has contributed significantly to a level of health that has made the Mormon community surprisingly more healthy than most other defined communities.

Q Is it true that Mormons don't drink alcohol or smoke tobacco?

Although there are always exceptions in any group, in general, Mormons abstain from drinking all forms of alcohol, and from using all forms of tobacco. This is why, in many groups (both youth and adult), it's relatively easy to spot the Mormons, for they're the ones abstaining. No wine at dinner; no beer at the ball game; no mixed drinks at the office party; no shots at the bar.

To many, this sounds insufferably boring and antisocial. But to Mormons, they'd rather avoid the barroom smoke, avoid the alcohol-related accidents (and family breakups), and save the thousands of dollars that smokers and drinkers spend each year on their "social" habits.

Q *Why don't Mormons drink coffee or tea?*

As mentioned elsewhere, Mormons don't drink coffee or tea because, in 1833, Joseph Smith claimed to have received a revelation from God commanding him to encourage the members of the Church to refrain from drinking alcohol, from smoking tobacco, and from drinking coffee and tea.

Most Mormons will politely pass when offered coffee or tea, although there are some Mormons who interpret the revelation to mean that they should avoid caffeine, and so there are some who will drink decaffeinated coffee or decaffeinated tea, or herbal teas that have no actual tea in them. But generally Mormons abstain from drinking coffee or tea on religious grounds.

In many cultures, not drinking coffee or tea (or even wine), would be unheard of. Many ask: "If they don't drink coffee, tea, or wine, what *do* they drink?" And the answer is just as boring as most people would guess: water, orange juice, milk, root beer, lemonade . . . and lots of hot chocolate.

Q Is it true that Mormons won't drink Coke or Pepsi?

Back in the 1830s, one of the revelations that Joseph Smith professed to have received from God is called *The Word of Wisdom*. This was a revelation outlining certain health habits that God counseled his followers—the members of His Church—to practice. Some of the counsel included: don't smoke tobacco, don't drink alcohol, and don't drink coffee or tea.

Over the years, many Mormons (and by observation of those members, many non-Mormons alike) have interpreted the coffee and tea reference to mean: don't take in any caffeine, as both coffee and tea contain high levels of caffeine. Furthermore, because most cola drinks, and many other products such as aspirin and chocolate, have caffeine in them, there are many Mormons who have avoided drinking Coke and other caffeinated beverages. The Word of Wisdom, however, does not mention caffeine by name, it merely mentions "hot drinks" (which the prophet later clarified as meaning coffee and tea), and goes on to encourage "moderation in all things."

During most people's interactions with Mormons, you'll find that there are some Mormons who are quite strong in their commitment to not drink caffeinated drinks, including Coke and Pepsi; and there are others who feel that the Word of Wisdom doesn't say not to drink caffeine, it just says not to drink coffee and tea. The fact is that you're apt to find Mormons who don't drink caffeinated soft drinks, Mormons who only drink caffeine-free soft drinks, and even Mormons who don't consider this much of an issue, either way, as long as they're not drinking coffee or tea.

13

MORMON ATTITUDES TOWARD MARRIAGE, FAMILIES, AND DIVORCE

Q *Is the Mormon Church family-oriented?*

Perhaps more than nearly any other church on earth, the Mormon Church holds up the family as the primary unit of society, both on earth and in heaven. As stated elsewhere, Mormons believe that Heavenly Father is married to a Heavenly Mother, and that, as parents, they had "spirit" children . . . and that all of the people who've ever lived on the face of the earth are literally the children of God, and brothers and sisters to each other.

Using this as a pattern, Mormons believe that the best way to raise children in this life, is for there to be a father and a mother, who have children whom they care for. This system—which they assert exists both throughout the eternities of heaven, as well as during this mortal life on earth—forms the basis of the Mormon Church's strong support of the individual family unit. And the fact is that most people's experience with Mormon families reveals them to be very close-knit, to have lots more contact with extended family members (such as grand-parents, aunts and uncles, and cousins), and to split up much less frequently than do families in most other groups.

Q *Where does the Mormon Church stand on traditional family values?*

The Mormon Church is a family-oriented church. And although there are Mormons who've been raised in single-parent families, and Mormon families that have gone through divorce, and certainly Mormon families who've experienced difficult times, in general, Mormon families are nuclear families—with a father, a mother, and a handful of children.

Mormons believe that everyone on earth preexisted in heaven as spirit children of God, and when they were born onto the earth, their spirits were united with a physical body to produce a mortal person. Mormons contend that each family that babies are born into represents a training ground for earthly mothers and fathers to develop the characteristics and Christ-like traits that Heavenly Mother and Heavenly Father have.

And therefore, according to Mormons, the basic training ground for all people is to be raised by their parents, with the father primarily serving as the provider and the mother primarily serving as the nurturer, but together they are serving as the counselors, leaders, helpers, friends, and loving parents of children, just as Heavenly Father and Heavenly Mother are the counselors, leaders, helpers, friends, and loving parents for all of us.

Given this as a baseline, Mormons are very strong on family values. They believe in the nuclear family; they believe in morality; they believe in being faithful to each other; they believe in families staying together, eating together, and doing things together; and they believe in children honoring their parents.

Mormons are usually community stalwarts when it comes

to traditional family values. They're often active in volunteer work, at the schools, in local politics, and with community service groups. Although there are divorces in Mormon families, the divorce rate is lower, the infidelity rate is much less, and there are a greater number of intact nuclear families than there are in the general population.

And because Mormons believe that every child is a distinct child of God, they are strong pro-life advocates, and are against abortion. Because of this, Mormons, like Catholics, tend to have larger families. As with the general population, there are some Mormon parents who are unable to have children, there are some who are only able to have one or two children, but it is not uncommon for some Mormon families to have five or more children in their families. This is quite different from the family sizes of most Protestant, Jewish, and other religious communities in the U.S. today.

Q *When many young couples these days have decided not to have children, or to have no more than two, why is it that Mormons have so many?*

Mormons believe that God (they generally refer to Him as *Heavenly Father*) has already created the spirits of all of His children who will ultimately be born on the earth. They further believe that there are a finite number of these spirit children, and that they will all be born before the end of the thousand-year Millennium of Christ's reign, which will occur after the Second Coming of Jesus Christ.

From this perspective, Mormons believe that parents have an obligation to provide a home for as many of God's children as the husband and wife have jointly determined to be the number that's best for their circumstances.

In like manner, they feel that if they unduly limit the size of their families, that the additional spirit children who were originally intended to join their families will be born into other families. From this viewpoint, Mormons feel that there is an obligation and a stewardship that rests upon those who have happy marriages and loving families to provide a safe and nurturing home to children who might otherwise be born into poverty or other difficult and dangerous circumstances around the world.

Given this belief, it's easy to see why Mormons are also against abortion (and all premarital and extramarital sex, for that matter), and to understand why they tend to not limit the size of their families through contraceptives and other means that are commonly in use these days. For this reason, in most neighborhoods around the world, it's not uncommon for people—when they see a large family—to assume that they must either be Catholic or Mormon, because those are generally the only two groups that still have large families.

Q Is it true that the divorce rate among Mormons is lower than most other groups?

It is true that, in general, Mormons have a lower divorce rate than most other groups. The primary reason for this is that worthy Mormons are married in their temples, as opposed to their local churches. Mormons believe that they have the authority from God to marry husbands and wives in their temples "for time and all eternity," not just until death do them part.

Therefore, to Mormons, temple marriages are even more sacred than civil marriages. They believe that (if they remain worthy), they will stay married even after they die and go to heaven . . . and that they'll be able to have their children together with them throughout all of the eternities.

In Mormon temple marriages, the husbands and wives make sacred covenants with each other—and with God—to not break their marriage vows. Because of this, Mormons tend to treat their marriage vows more seriously, and tend to be more focused on making their marriages work successfully, than on looking for reasons why it may not work out. Divorce is still possible for Mormons, but it is discouraged, and requires both partners to go through a number of soul-searching steps (unless infidelity, abuse, or some criminal activity is involved).

Q How do Mormons manage to keep their families together?

Even though Mormon families may have a higher rate of intact, two-parent families than the national average, don't assume that all Mormon families are perfect, or without problems. As with families everywhere, there are daily trials, financial struggles, occasional wayward kids, and the life-long challenge of trying to make a marriage work.

But Mormon families often do have the additional advantages of daily prayer; active Church support; a commitment to complete marital fidelity; no alcohol usage; no swearing, smoking, or drug abuse; an at-home mom to provide around-the-clock supervision, homework monitoring, and sit-down meals around the kitchen table; and the acclaimed Mormon family-togetherness program, called Family Home Evening.

First introduced back in 1915, and officially established as a Mormon Church program in 1965, Family Home Evening was the name given to a weekly family-togetherness night (usually held on Monday nights), during which all family members set aside their own projects and responsibilities, and come together for an hour or so to play games, hold a family council (to plan out the week's activities and transportation needs), discuss each other's successes and struggles for that week, pray together, laugh together, have refreshments (it wouldn't be Mormon without refreshments), and have a faith-promoting lesson that encourages service, charity, kindness, righteous behavior, or some other Christ-centered Gospel principle.

One of the recent Mormon prophets, David O. McKay, taught Church members that "No success can compensate for failure in the home." This simple advice from a prophet of the Lord, has served as a touchstone for Mormons for nearly forty years; and, coupled with the admonition for each family to hold Family Home Evening regularly each week, and the Church's 1995 official Proclamation to the World regarding the importance of the family and keeping families together, has given Mormon Church members the tools needed to help them more successfully keep their families together.

Over the years, the Mormon Church's Family Home Evening program has been recognized worldwide for its positive impact on individual family members, on keeping families together, and on strengthening local communities. And Mormons everywhere are glad to share their family night program ideas, lesson manuals, and experiences with others—even those who have no interest in joining their Church—who would like to reap the benefits of this effective family-building program.

Q What is the Mormon attitude toward education?

Mormons are strong believers in education. They believe that the family is the cornerstone of society, and that each family should be self-sufficient. And one of the key ways for any family to earn enough money to pay for their family's needs, is for the parents to be college educated and to be able to have a successful professional career.

In this regard, Mormons often attempt to raise their children to do well in school. And many Mormon parents encourage their children to go on to college and beyond. There are many Mormons who become doctors and lawyers and businesspeople; but there are, of course, those who would be much happier and more successful working on a farm, or in manual labor, or as skilled tradesmen . . . such as electricians, plumbers, mechanics, and computer operators. Overall, Mormons are believers in learning what the world has developed, but always within the context of the truth of the Gospel of Jesus Christ.

Q   *What is the Mormon attitude toward employment?*

Mormons believe that every father should be gainfully employed in order to support his wife and children. Mormons do not believe in the dole (or government welfare); however, they do have a very strong Church welfare program, which helps those who are faced with unemployment or other difficult times or emergency situations.

There are, of course, exceptional family circumstances that might require the mother to work—owing to the absence or the loss of the father (whether by divorce, illness, or death)—at which point the mother becomes the breadwinner for the family. But in general, Mormons believe that it's the parents who are responsible to earn a living that's sufficient to provide for the needs of their children; and typically, Mormons are hardworking, successful people who do just that.

Q Do Mormons feel that some occupations are more honorable or better than others?

No. Mormons are much more focused on whether or not a man is a good husband and a good father, than they are on what he does for a living, and how much money he makes. All honest work is respected by the Mormon faith, and Mormons are believers that a man or woman should put in an honest day's work for the pay he or she receives.

Although they advocate getting as much education and training as possible, in order to be able to enter a profession that will provide adequately for the family, Mormons contend that the world is just as much in need of good auto mechanics as it is in need of good lawyers, and that it needs more at-home moms to raise better-behaved children than it needs families with three cars, three TVs, three computers, but with children who aren't doing very well in school, and often getting into trouble.

They claim that when everyone faces the judgment seat in heaven, Jesus won't ask them what profession they had, or how much money they made. Mormons think He'll ask them. "Were they honest in all their dealings?" "Did they treat everyone with kindness and charity?" "Did they love their spouse and children, and provide for their physical, spiritual, and emotional needs?" To Mormons, these are the issues that are much more important than what someone's occupation is.

Q   *What do the inside of Mormon churches look like?*

Mormon chapel buildings are just like most Christian church buildings. There's a sanctuary; there are classrooms for Sunday School, a nursery, and other small-group meetings; and there are offices for the local minister (the bishop) and his assistants. Architecturally, most Mormon chapels (as opposed to Mormon temples) are quite plain. Occasionally you'll see some stained-glass windows in some of the older buildings; but for the most part, money is spent frugally, so that more lower-cost chapels can be built, rather than fewer, fancier ones. Mormons use their chapel buildings as their weekly houses of worship, to sing hymns, and to conduct their Sabbath day and other weekly meetings.

Although Mormon chapels usually have a steeple, and often look quite similar to most other Christian churches, there is not a cross on top. Because Mormons focus more on the Resurrection of Jesus Christ, rather than on His Crucifixion, they do not routinely use the cross, which is the most commonly recognized Christian symbol.

Typically, the large central area in a Mormon church has accordion-style wall dividers that permit the chapel portion to be enlarged, allowing more people to attend. As you might expect, there are pews, a pulpit, and a table for preparing the Sacrament. Often the extended part of the central area, that is not normally used for the chapel, houses basketball hoops and volleyball nets, and all of the typical paraphernalia for a gymnasium . . . to permit the youth of each congregation to play basketball and other sports, once the room dividers have been closed and the folding chairs taken down.

As people travel around the world and see Mormon chapels, often they will realize that they are all very similar to one another. This is primarily because (unlike most churches, where the local congregation raises money and builds its own building), all Mormon members pay tithes, and the tithing goes to Church headquarters, and is then redistributed to where new chapel buildings are needed.

And therefore, when a new Mormon chapel building is built, it is paid for, in full, by the accumulated tithing funds of those throughout the world. There are no mortgages on Mormon churches. The land is purchased, the building is constructed as inexpensively (but with as high quality as possible), and, in order to help keep costs down, the same architectural models are often used over and over again.

Q Why do Mormons have temples, when other Christian churches don't?

Mormons have temples because they believe God told them to have temples. Joseph Smith claimed to have been instructed by God (through revelation) to build temples. The Mormons built their first temple in Kirkland, Ohio, in 1836, which they had to abandon when they were run out of town by anti-Mormons. (This building still stands, and is open to the public, although no longer owned by the Church.)

The Mormons built their second temple in Nauvoo, Illinois, which was also abandoned when they were run out of town, again by anti-Mormons. This temple was burned to the ground by mob protestors. (It is now being reconstructed, and will be completed in 2002.) The Mormons then made their way by wagon train to Salt Lake City (led by Brigham Young, who succeeded Joseph Smith after he was murdered), and built a number of temples in Utah. The Salt Lake Temple, which is perhaps the most famous, was completed in 1893, and is still in operation.

Mormons build temples because they claim God told them to, just as God told Solomon to build a temple: to perform sacred ordinances for worthy members; to perform Baptisms for those who have died; to perform eternal marriages and "sealings" that connect families together—husband to wife, and parents to children—that can secure them beyond the grave, so that families can be together eternally, and not just "until death do them part."

Most Christians feel that temples were an Old Testament component of Judaism, and do not share the Mormon belief that the Jewish faith is merely one of the Twelve Tribes of Israel, and that all twelve tribes were really Christian. In the absence of this novel perspective, Protestants and Catholics do not see temples as a part of their religious services.

Mormons have a very different understanding and interpretation of these issues. They feel that God has *one* Plan of Salvation and *one* Church, and that it was the same Church that was given to Adam and all of the prophets in the Old Testament; it was the same Church that Jesus Christ established and clarified and corrected when he was on earth; it was the same Church presided over by Paul and the Apostles until they were all killed or died; and it's the same Church that was restored by Joseph Smith. As you can see, for Mormons, their temples are sacred, special edifices, and not just buildings where their Sunday worship services are held.

There are, of course, some small Christian churches that do not have national or international affiliations who use the term *temple* for their local church buildings, and who have their own interpretation of the meaning of that term. But that is quite different from the Mormon belief.

Q It seems suspicious that non-Mormons aren't allowed inside Mormon temples. What secret things go on in there?

The few groups that are hostile toward Mormons make a special effort to claim that there are secret, suspicious, and probably "satanic" things that go on inside Mormon temples. Mormons, of course, would explain it quite differently. They would say that the things that go on in Mormon temples are so sacred, that they do not want them defiled by those who would mock them or make light of them, and therefore they don't discuss them in public.

Mormons believe that their temple ceremonies are the same ceremonies that were performed by all the prophets of old, wherever temples have existed, and that these are special ceremonies (Mormons call them sacred ordinances) that need to be performed by members of the Church who are serious about the covenants they have made with God. They feel that they are merely obeying God's commandments by going to the temple often to perform these important ordinances for the benefit of themselves, their families, and their ancestors.

There is nothing unusual or bizarre about the ordinances that go on inside Mormon temples. There are marriages, Baptisms for those who've died, and educational sessions . . . during which members make covenants with God. These observances are sacred religious ordinances that Mormons believe God instituted to help ensure that families can return to heaven and be together forever.

However, in what may come as a surprise to many non-Mormons, their temples are *not* where they hold their Sunday worship services. Whereas Mormons have more than one hundred temples worldwide, they have more than twelve thousand local chapels—buildings in which local congregations meet and hold their Sabbath day services, their Sunday School, their choir practices, their youth meetings, and so on—and those buildings are open to anyone who would like to visit.

However, entrance to Mormon temples, because of their sacred nature, is limited to those who are active members of the Church and have passed an annual interview with their local bishop . . . at which time they reaffirm their faith and their beliefs, they acknowledge their weaknesses, and establish their worthiness to enter the temple. And because only worthy members of the Church are permitted to enter the temple, the Mormon Church will often have a visitors' center for the general public, right on temple grounds, where people who are curious about what goes on in the temple can visit, can see photographs of the interior, can be taught why Mormons have temples and what goes on inside them, so that they can get as much information as they would like and not feel that they are being denied anything about Mormon beliefs.

Q

If they claim to be Christians, why are Mormon temples closed on Sundays?

Many faiths use the word *temple* to refer to their chapels, meetinghouses, or church buildings. In the case of the Mormons, however, their temples are not where they hold their weekly worship services. Their weekly meetinghouses are called chapels, which *are* open on Sundays, and which are where Mormons go for worship services, to partake of the Sacrament of the Last Supper, and to have their Sunday School and other weekly Church meetings.

Mormon temples are very different from local congregational meetinghouses. They consider them to be sacred buildings where special ordinances of the Gospel are performed, which are distinct and separate from the weekly Sacrament meetings. Because Mormons are expected to attend their weekly worship services in their local chapels, their temples are closed on Sundays (and normally on Mondays, as well); however, they are open Tuesdays through Saturdays. This is why the parking lots in Mormon temples are empty on Sundays (which is often confusing to the casual observer), because the Sunday worship services are not held in temples, they are held in thousands of Mormon chapels around the world.

MORMON CLERGY

Q *How is it possible that the Mormons have no paid ministers, or choir directors, or Sunday School teachers, or any of those positions that are salaried at most other churches?*

It comes as a major surprise to most people, but the Mormon Church is entirely run by unpaid volunteers. There are no paid positions within the ecclesiastic leadership of the Mormon Church. In Mormonism, a local congregation is led by a bishop, who is called by the stake president, who is called by a regional authority, who is called by the Twelve Apostles, who are chosen by the prophet, who is selected, according to Mormon belief, by Jesus Christ Himself, through revelation.

The local bishop might be a farmer or a businessman, a dentist or a garbage collector. He keeps his full-time job, he keeps his role as husband and father in his family; but on top of that, for a period of about five years, he serves as the spiritual leader of the local congregation.

The local congregation (Mormons call them *wards*) is run by similarly called volunteers, who lead the choir, teach Sunday School, teach the Primary children, set up the chairs, clean the building . . . who, in all aspects, care for the local church, the local church facilities, and all of its members. All of these people serve on a voluntary basis and no one gets paid.

This is quite different from nearly all other churches, where the weekly passing of the offering plate provides the funds that pay the salary of all of these people . . . along with the heating bill, the air-conditioning bill, the car allowance, the health insurance for the minister, and the other paid positions in their churches. None of that occurs in a Mormon Church. This is why, if you meet a Mormon, you should ask them what their current *calling* is, and they will list one or two (or three or four) different jobs in the local Church that they are doing, on top of their other household and employment duties.

Q *What is a bishop in the Mormon Church? In the*
   Catholic Church, the bishop is a very high
   position; is that the same in the Mormon Church?

Actually, in the Mormon Church, the term *bishop* merely refers to the local minister or pastor for each congregation, and therefore the traditions are quite different. In a Catholic Church, your local pastor might be the priest; in a Protestant church, it might be a pastor or minister; in a Jewish synagogue, it might be a rabbi; but in a Mormon Church, the term *bishop* is the one used for the local minister. A Mormon bishop has two counselors, and the three of them form the core leadership of the local congregation, which Mormons call the *bishopric*.

The hierarchy in the Mormon Church is really quite structured; there is a prophet (who Mormons believe is selected by Jesus Christ and called by God), who is the president of the Church. He selects two counselors (assistants), and the three of them form what is called the First Presidency of the Church. The next level down is the Quorum of the Twelve Apostles. As in Christ's time, the Mormon Church has twelve Apostles, and they make up what Mormons refer to as the Quorum of the Twelve Apostles. The First Presidency and the Quorum of Twelve represent the top leadership of the Mormon Church.

Under the Twelve, there are then several groups of priesthood holders, called Quorums of Seventy, which consist of senior church leaders who represent the prophet and the Apostles, and who travel around the world to bring counsel to local leaders, and to take the concerns of those leaders back to Church headquarters. These people meet with the local leaders, and then meet periodically with the First Presidency and the Quorum of the Twelve, to arrange the affairs of the Church.

These members of the Quorums of Seventy are organized internationally into threesomes (again with one serving as president, and two serving as counselors), which are in charge of various geographic areas. These threesomes are called area presidencies; and under the area presidencies are the local stakes, and each stake typically has five to ten local congregations, or wards. The stakes each have a president and two counselors, making up the stake presidency, and then each ward has a bishop with two counselors, making up the bishopric.

The prophet and his counselors pray for and seek revelation as to who should be called to the Apostleship when someone dies. The Quorum of the Twelve Apostles and the First Presidency pray for and seek revelation on who should be called to serve on the Quorums of Seventy, and then these general authorities (in their local areas where they are assigned as area presidents) pray for and seek revelation as to who should be the local stake presidents. Each stake president then seeks, through prayer and revelation, who he should call to be his counselors, which have to be approved from above. The stake presidencies then pray for and seek counsel on who should be the bishops of each local congregation.

At the local level, the bishop is the minister for the local ward; he is in charge of the Sunday services and the priesthood, the various auxiliary organizations of the Church—the Sunday School, the choir, the youth program, the Primary Organization children's programs, and so on—but has the help of an elaborate organization of other volunteer workers. The bishop and his counselors, and the other organization leaders in each congregation, pray for guidance and revelation on who should be the choir director, who should teach which Sunday School class, who should be the Young Women's Organization head, and who should be the Young Men's Organization head, and so on.

Wards typically have from two hundred to four hundred members, and in most cases, every one of those members (who's at least eighteen years old), has some kind of a calling or volunteer position in the Church, and they all work together as an organized unit to carry out the programs of the Church at the local level. When membership in a ward reaches around five hundred people, it is split into two wards, so that each local congregation doesn't get too large and unmanageable for its volunteer leadership, and so that every member has the opportunity to serve in a calling. (Unlike some Christian congregations, where local membership sometimes exceeds several thousand people and the weekly contributions are sufficient to build large and elaborate church buildings, the Mormons intentionally limit the size of each congregation, and often even have two or three local wards sharing a single building . . . with one ward meeting from say, 9:00 A.M. till noon on Sundays, and another meeting from 1:00 to 4:00 P.M. on those same Sundays.)

Q **Some Protestant Churches have the position of Deacon. Are there similar positions in the Mormon Church?**

Actually, there are similar positions, but they are not called deacons; and there are Deacons, but they are not in similar positions. In the Mormon Church, because there is a lay ministry (unpaid and not educated at theological schools), the bishop, his counselors, and the other local leaders form a council called the ward correlation council, and they organize and coordinate all of the activities at the local ward. At the stake level, there is a stake high council, which is made up of the stake presidency and a group of twelve high counselors, who represent members from the local congregations within the stake, and who provide support and counsel to the decisions at the local and stake level. That group of people functions in much the same capacity as do the deacons, or adult senior leaders, at some other churches.

In the Mormon Church, the term *Deacon* is also used, but it denotes a very different calling. There are two levels of priesthood in the Mormon Church. The *Aaronic Priesthood,* named after Aaron (who was Moses' assistant and spokesperson), and the *Melchizedek Priesthood,* named after Melchizedek (who was the high priest in the Bible to whom Abraham paid tithes).

These two levels of priesthood have callings within them. The Aaronic Priesthood is primarily the preparatory priesthood for young men ages twelve through seventeen who are learning the duties of service and leadership in the Church, and who will be given the Melchizedek Priesthood once they are worthy, and have reached the age of eighteen. Among the Aaronic Priesthood, those who are twelve and thirteen are ordained to the office of *Deacon,* and that is the first level in the Aaronic Priesthood for young men. Once they turn fourteen, they are ordained to the office of *Teacher* in the Aaronic Priesthood; and once they become sixteen, they are ordained to the office of *Priest,* still within the Aaronic Priesthood.

The Melchizedek Priesthood has two levels in it. The first is the office of *Elder,* and all worthy Mormon men eighteen and older have the Melchizedek Priesthood conferred upon them, and they are ordained to the office of Elder in the Church. And once they have considerable experience in leadership positions, and are in their forties and fifties, many are then ordained to the office of *High Priest* in the Melchizedek Priesthood.

Q I've heard that Mormons believe that they have a
prophet on the earth today. Is that true? And is it
true that Mormons believe that they have twelve
Apostles on earth, just like the Apostle Paul and
the others in Jesus' time?

Mormons do believe that they have a prophet on earth today. Mormons refer to the Book of Amos in the Old Testament, where the prophet said: *"Surely the Lord God will do
nothing, but he revealeth his secret unto his servants the prophets."* (Amos 3:7) Mormons believe that The Church of Jesus
Christ was the Church Adam and Eve belonged to. And
that Noah and Abraham and Moses and all of the Biblical
prophets were the chosen leaders, in their time, of the
Church of Jesus Christ.

When Jesus Christ came, he chose twelve Apostles. No
prophet was needed, because the Son of God Himself was
here; but He called twelve Apostles, who were the second
tier of leadership in the Church, and they communicated
to all the local Church leaders in each of the cities where
there was a community of Saints. So Paul, being an Apostle,
communicated with the Saints in Corinth, and the Saints
in Ephesus, and the Saints in Rome, and the Saints in Thes-
salonica, and so on.

Mormons believe that this is the pattern that God has
always used with His Church. Mormons believe that, after
all of the Apostles were killed or died, God withdrew His
priesthood from the earth, and left mankind without a
prophet . . . until He and Jesus appeared to Joseph Smith in
1820. Mormons believe that they called him to be the
prophet for these "latter days" (the days nearest the Second
Coming of Jesus Christ), and to restore the priesthood and
The Church of Jesus Christ to the earth. They believe that

Joseph Smith was the first prophet of the latter days, and (as he was instructed to do by God) that he selected twelve Apostles by revelation and inspiration from Jesus Christ.

Upon Joseph Smith's murder, these Apostles then carefully prayed for divine guidance and inspiration, and received a revelation to call Brigham Young to be the next prophet. Brigham Young then led the "Latter-day Saints" to Salt Lake City. Since that time there have been many such prophets, and as of the writing of this book, President Gordon B. Hinckley is the current prophet of The Church of Jesus Christ of Latter-day Saints.

The Mormon Church is run by this prophet, who claims to receive revelations from Jesus Christ and God the Father, and acts under Christ's own direction, in anticipation of the Second Coming.

Now, there are some other religions and churches and denominations that claim that they, too, have had a prophet. Muslims believe in Mohammed; Buddhists believe in Buddha; some Asian religions believe in Confucius; and some Christian Scientists believe that Mary Baker Eddy was a prophet. But most American mainstream Protestant Church leaders do not believe in prophets . . . they believe that prophets were done away with in the Old Testament, and that once Jesus arrived, there were no longer prophets to run the Church, merely local ministers and pastors.

Q Most Christian ministers have been ordained after going to theological school. What qualifies Mormon bishops to serve as ministers? And by what authority do they claim the right to preach the Gospel of Jesus Christ?

This is one of those significant differences that separate Mormonism from most other Christian churches. It's true that most Christian denominations—both Catholic and Protestant—have theological schools for those interested in pursuing the ministry. After graduating from college, aspiring pastors attend such schools in order to study for the ministry and receive a Doctor of Divinity degree. Most such graduates are usually ordained by the college they've attended, at which point certain denominations and local churches will recruit them to serve in their congregations. Once ordained in this fashion, most ministers can apply for jobs with different churches—and even different denominations—across the country.

The Mormon ministry is entirely different. There is no religiously trained clergy in the Mormon Church; there are no theological schools; and there are no special programs to train people to be qualified as ministers. Quite the opposite is true. Because of their core belief that each individual family represents the most important unit of any society, Mormons believe that God wants every single family to have its own minister.

How is this possible? In order to understand Mormonism's solution to this challenge, one must go back to the Joseph Smith story for clarification.

Mormons believe that Jesus Himself taught His prophet Joseph about the importance of Baptism; and that, while prayerfully seeking how one would get the authority to baptize, Joseph Smith stated that he was visited by John the Baptist (on assignment from Jesus Christ), who placed his hands on Joseph's head and bestowed upon him the *Aaronic Priesthood,* which gave him the authority to perform Baptisms in the name of Jesus Christ.

A few months later, Joseph Smith declared that Peter, James, and John—three of the original Twelve Apostles of Jesus Christ—also visited him (in angelic form), and placed their hands upon his head and bestowed upon him the *Melchizedek Priesthood,* which gave him the authority to perform all of the other administrations pertaining to the Gospel of Jesus Christ.

Mormons assert that these two priesthoods—given to Joseph Smith, and through him to others—represent the heavenly authorization to preach the Gospel of Jesus Christ (and the same authorization that prophets have always had). All male members of the Mormon Church, once they have been determined, through interview, to be worthy, are ordained to offices within these two priesthoods. At twelve, they have the Aaronic (or preparatory) Priesthood conferred upon them; and then, at eighteen or older, they have the Melchizedek Priesthood conferred upon them.

In this way, a twelve-year-old boy in the Mormon Church can be ordained a Deacon in the Aaronic Priesthood, and an eighteen-year-old young man can be ordained an Elder in the Melchizedek Priesthood. Once they have the priesthood, they then have the authorization, with the approval of their local congregation's bishop, to perform the appropriate ordinances in the Mormon Church. Therefore, with this priesthood authority, Baptisms can be performed, the Gift of the Holy Ghost can be bestowed after Baptisms, and other ministerial duties can be conducted.

With every male member being an ordained priesthood

holder, almost every family has a minister in their home. And for those that do not—widows, divorced mothers, and single women—the Mormon Church provides an elaborate organization—called *Home Teaching*—that sends a pair of priesthood holders to visit every single Mormon household every single month. Thus, for Mormons, all of the ministerial duties are performed by unpaid male members of the Church throughout the world. The local bishop may serve as the ecclesiastical leader of the local congregation, but most local congregations will have approximately fifty to one hundred priesthood holders, who all have the authority to minister in the Gospel of Jesus Christ.

This is quite a different organization than that which exists in most Christian denominations. And this is what is referred to as the "lay ministry" of the Mormon Church. No one is formally trained; no one is paid; all men who are worthy are given the priesthood; and the various leaders prayerfully seek revelation and inspiration from God as to who should be called to the many positions that keep a local congregation functioning. Men are called to priesthood positions; women are called to positions of leadership in the Sunday School, in the Relief Society (the world's largest women's organization), in the Young Women's Organization (for teenagers), and in the Primary Organization (which is for children under twelve).

Q *A lot of churches are just started by a minister who feels called to organize a church. How are Mormon Churches started?*

Mormon congregations are formed wherever Mormons are living. For some churches, a minister decides to start a church, and then proceeds to try to recruit members. For Mormons, it's just the reverse. A body of members exists within some geographic boundary, and Church headquarters organizes them into a local congregation or *ward* . . . and then the local stake president calls a *bishop* from among the members of the congregation. Remember, for Mormons, bishops are called from among the local membership; there are no ministers who ask to be assigned to certain congregations, nor would they have the authority to establish their own wards.

16 WHAT DO MORMONS BELIEVE?

Q *What do Mormons think the purpose of life is?*

Mormons have a very visionary view of what life is all about . . . about why the earth was created; about why there are people here; and about what our purpose is. And, while most scholars and atheists claim that there is no intrinsic purpose to life, that it is random happenstance that the earth is here and that we happen to be on it, Mormons have quite a different view.

It is their view that there is a God in heaven, and that He is the Creator of all things. Mormons believe that one of His greatest and most cherished creations are His children—us. They believe that He had created His children, in spirit form, and that they lived with Him in heaven before the earth was created. As they began to grow and develop, Mormons contend that they wanted to grow up to be like Him (in the same way that all little children want to grow up to be like their parents).

Mormons assert, however, that God the Father had a physical body, in addition to being a spirit. And that He was a righteous God, while they were still children and did not have the character traits needed to become like Him. They believe that God wanted His children to be happy (and the greatest happiness was living with Him in the Celestial Kingdom of heaven forever), but that only righteous people who have resurrected bodies could live in the Celestial Kingdom of heaven, and that, therefore, they must get a body and qualify to develop the traits that God the Father has.

The Mormon view is that God the Father, and His Son, Jesus Christ, laid forth the great Plan of Salvation, which called for an earth to be created, where His spirit children could be born into human bodies (patterned after Heavenly Father's body, both male and female), and where they would have the opportunity to learn how to live righteously—while they confront the many trials and difficulties that they would have to face—and be tested as to whether or not they could develop God-like, Christ-like traits.

However, Mormons believe that a key part of the plan was that God would place a "veil" between His children on earth and their memory of where they came from, thus forcing them to develop these God-like traits on their own—based on faith and a desire to do what is right—rather than on the sure knowledge that they wouldn't qualify to return home to heaven unless they lived righteous lives. To Mormons, having faith is to believe in what's on the other side of the veil—that God lives, that Jesus Christ can forgive sins that have been repented of, and that a glorious resurrection lies beyond the grave, where families can return "home" to live with Heavenly Father again.

Therefore, from the Mormon perspective, the purpose of life on earth is to learn to live by faith, and to develop the

Christ-like qualities that will qualify a person to return to heaven and live with God.

In their view, there are two absolutes here: on the one hand, once on earth, all humans would commit sin of one kind or another, and become "unclean"; while on the other hand, no unclean thing could live with God. These two truths seem to seal the fate of all of mankind . . . they were doomed from the beginning to be denied access to heaven.

But because, according to Mormons, the whole purpose of the Plan of Salvation was to provide such access, they believe that God sent His Son, Jesus Christ, to *atone* for the sins of mankind, and to provide a way for them to repent of their sins and have them washed away . . . so that they would no longer be unclean.

Mormons believe that the Lord Jesus Christ is the Savior of the world, and is integral to the reason we have a life on earth. They feel that God hopes all of His children will choose to take advantage of the Savior's sacrifice and Atonement. Mormons believe that all people will be resurrected after this life (*"For as in Adam all die, even so in Christ shall all be made alive."* 1 Corinthians 15:22), but that not all will be given the opportunity to live at the highest level of heaven, with God the Father, because—although immortality is a free gift from Jesus Christ—living with Heavenly Father is contingent upon righteousness and good behavior.

To wrap it up, Mormons believe that we are here on earth to gain bodies—which we all have done—but also to qualify for the highest level of heaven, which is contingent upon our behavior. To them, the purpose of life is to learn to live righteously, in spite of all of the trials and tribulations that come our way. To endure to the end is the goal. To gain eternal joy and happiness is what Heavenly Father has in mind for all of His children; but because they get to choose for themselves, Mormons believe that God gives all the help that He can, without lifting the veil (which would negate the need for faith). He answers prayers; He has provided us with the Holy Scriptures (both the Bible and the Book of Mormon), with prophets, with parents, with the Church, with the Holy Ghost; He has done everything that He could possibly do to encourage people to get on the right path and work out their own salvation with the benefit of the grace of the Lord Jesus Christ.

From this perspective, Mormons believe that all people came to earth from heaven, having already been born as spirit children of God; that all of mankind are brothers and sisters; that our purpose here is to find the Church, to live righteously, to take advantage of Christ's Atonement and sacrifice (and the opportunity to have our sins forgiven and cleansed); and then to return, after death, to the glorious resurrection and to eternal life with Heavenly Father and Jesus Christ.

Q *Most religions are pretty vague, or claim that it's a mystery, about what the ultimate Plan of Salvation is. Do Mormons have some particular explanation of Christ's Plan of Salvation?*

Yes, Mormons have a rather comprehensive view of the Plan of Salvation. They believe that it was Heavenly Father's original intent to try to get all of His spirit children to return home to Him. But Mormons believe that, in order to dwell in the highest degree of heaven, only resurrected spirit children, who have received a body and who have earned their way through their own faith and behavior ("works"), can qualify to live at the highest level.

Therefore it is their belief that the earth was created so that all of God's children could receive a body; but, because a *veil* has been drawn, which hides the existence of heaven from the people on earth, they also believe that people have to live their earthly, mortal existence, without the knowledge of heaven . . . and therefore they must operate on faith and learn to live righteously through their own free agency.

This is how Mormons interpret God's "testing" of His children on earth. This is the probationary period of a person's life. To Mormons, this is the reason the earth exists. They believe that everyone will be resurrected through Christ's Resurrection, but that they will only qualify for the highest level of glory in the Celestial Kingdom of heaven based on their behavior while on the earth.

Mormons then believe that all humans will die, thus ending their mortal life . . . but that all will continue to live on, spiritually, until their bodies are eventually resurrected and reunited with their spirits. They will then be judged by the Savior, the Lord Jesus Christ, based on their own behavior in this life. According to Mormons, if they heard the Gospel while on earth, understood its principles, and were accountable for living them, then how well they followed those principles will determine their ultimate judgment from God. Mormons are strong believers in the Golden Rule—that how they judge others will be how Jesus Christ will judge them.

For those who have not joined The Church of Jesus Christ of Latter-day Saints, or have never heard about Jesus Christ, Mormons believe that they will not be held accountable, and, once they've died and gone to heaven, they'll remain in a waiting or holding area (as they have not yet been baptized), where they will await missionaries to visit them. This is what most Catholics call *limbo,* what most Protestants call *paradise,* and what most Mormons refer to as *spirit prison.* Mormons believe that these are the "prisoners" that Christ preached to after his Resurrection (1 Peter 3:19–20). Mormons believe that those who die without having had the opportunity to learn the Gospel, will go to this spirit prison, and will there await the opportunity to learn more about the Gospel, and still have free agency to decide to join Christ's Church or not.

Mormons believe that there are many different levels of heaven, with the lowest still being more wonderful than life on earth, but not nearly as wonderful as where Heavenly Father (and Heavenly Mother) and Jesus Christ live. Mormons claim that attempting to achieve this highest level of exaltation represents ultimate happiness, and is the reason that Heavenly Father created His children in the first place. They believe that it's His hope that they will all qualify to return back to be with Him forever.

In this regard, the Mormon understanding of the Plan of Salvation is that we are here to learn to be as Christ-like as we can—to repent of our sins, to be washed clean, and to qualify to return home to live with our Heavenly Parents. In the Mormon view, what we do on earth, as a career, is next to irrelevant . . . it's how we live our life, how we treat our neighbors, how we treat our spouse, how we treat our children, how honest and true and Christ-like we've become, how honorably we've repented of the many mistakes we've each made, and how well we've attempted to endure in righteousness till the end. Mormons believe that those who do so, will achieve a wonderful blessing . . . everything that God has will be given to them. But for those who fall short—as with the rich man in one of the parables that Jesus taught (see Luke 16:19–31)—a "great gulf" will be fixed, and they will not be able to progress to the highest level of heaven.

As is apparent, the Mormon view of the Plan of Salvation is a very hopeful one, for it lays open the promise that everyone can qualify . . . if they repent of their sins and make wise choices. And nearly all sins can be repented of—that's why Jesus took upon Himself all the sins of the world. Of course, the sins of murder and of blasphemy against the truth, once received, are serious sins and difficult to be granted forgiveness for; and yet Mormons believe that there is hope for all, and, in fact, this is why Mormons have temples . . . to perform Baptisms and other ordinances for all the millions of people who have lived on the earth and have never heard of Jesus Christ, have never been taught the Gospel, and therefore have never had the opportunity to repent or be forgiven, to join the true Church or receive the priesthood, or to have those other ordinances performed for them.

Mormons believe that these people are every bit as important to Heavenly Father. He loves them, and has provided a way for them to also gain eternal life and exaltation, through the work that is done for them (by proxy, in the temple), after they have died. They are waiting for that work to be done, while they are in spirit prison.

Q *A lot of people think that there is no such thing as absolute truth, and that churches are just sort of trying to encourage people to be better. What do Mormons think about that? Is there such a thing as actual truth?*

It is true that most Christian churches no longer focus on absolute truth. While most still believe that Jesus existed historically, and that the Biblical account of His life and Resurrection really happened, many Christian denominations only teach about Jesus in very general terms. And there are considerable doctrinal differences between many denominations . . . with some believing, for instance, in Baptism by immersion, some in Baptism by sprinkling, and some even believing that Baptism is no longer required. Some believe that Baptisms can be performed by anyone, some believe that they can only be performed by ordained ministers, while others believe that ordinations from theological seminaries are not necessarily on authority from God. Mormons are puzzled by all these differences, citing Ephesians 4:5, where the Apostle Paul refers to *"One Lord, one faith, one baptism."*

There are similar differences between many different religions. There are Jewish congregations that still look forward to the coming of the Messiah; but there are others that no longer believe that the Messiah will ever come. There are Catholics who believe that the Catholic Church is God's official Church; but there are others who feel that it is merely trying to represent God's position as best as it can, but that there is probably no ongoing revelation received by its leaders.

And now, as mankind moves into the third millennium after Christ's birth, it's obvious that the members of most churches are merely trying to understand their religion as best they can. They get very little counsel on how to live righteously in a world that tends to mock most religious beliefs; and most ministers don't even claim to represent "truth," but merely encourage people to follow the basic principles as they interpret them from the Old and New Testaments.

Mormons take a different approach. They claim that these kinds of doctrinal differences were the very reasons that God withdrew the true Church (and His priesthood authority) from the earth after Christ's Apostles were all killed or died (see Matthew 21:23–46). And because the people on the earth were looking for the truth, but couldn't find it, the Catholic Church was then established . . . and then the Lutheran Church spun off from that, and then the Methodist Church, and the Dutch Reformed Church, and the Anglicans, and all of the various Protestant religions that were spin-offs from the Catholics . . . and that all of these represented individual efforts to rethink what was Christ's true Church, and to attempt to establish it as best they could.

Although well-meaning, Mormons believe that God had not given any of them the authority to lead the Church in His name; that none of them possessed the true priesthood of God; and that a *restoration* was necessary, led by God Himself. And that's part of the reason why Mormons believe in the Joseph Smith story, because they believe that it was God Himself, and Jesus Christ, who appeared to Joseph as a young boy, and said to him something like: "If you remain worthy, we will use you to restore the true Church; you will serve as the prophet of the restoration, and will reestablish Christ's Church on the earth, under Our direction."

In this regard, Mormons do believe that God has a specific Plan of Salvation, and a specific set of doctrines that are true and unchanging. They believe that most other churches have a portion of the truth—the Old Testament, the New Testament, the benefits of answers to prayers—but that they do not have God's priesthood or prophets, and therefore do not have the entirety of the truth.

Of course, there are some members of other faiths who consider it arrogant for Mormons to think this way. But doesn't everyone think that their church is God's true Church . . . otherwise, why would they join it? Mormons, in general, certainly try not to come across as arrogant (and most are very humble in the faithful adherence to their own Church doctrines), they just feel they are trying to do what's right. In fact, most Mormons are very tolerant and understanding of other faiths, and are grateful that other people are also trying to live righteous lives. Likewise, most members of other faiths are quite positive and tolerant—and even supportive—of the dedicated commitment that most Mormons have toward their own faith.

But there is a small pocket of ministers of certain Christian denominations (primarily fundamentalist and evangelical churches), who are quite hostile to Mormons, and who feel that Mormons are not Christian, are not representing Jesus Christ, and are not helping people to live righteous lives. Mormons answer that by saying: "You don't have to join our church, you don't have to believe what we believe. We merely ask that if people are curious, that they read the Book of Mormon, and after they've read it, to pray about it, and ask Heavenly Father if this book is true Scripture or not . . . and if it strengthens the reader's faith in the Lord Jesus Christ."

Mormons would then say that if—based on God's answers to those prayers—these people feel that the Book of Mormon is true, that they should then consider learning more about the Mormon Church. Similarly, if they feel that they didn't get an answer to their prayers, then Mormons would merely be glad that they took the opportunity to read the Book of Mormon, and wish them well.

Q Do Mormons believe in heaven?

Yes. Mormons not only believe in heaven but they believe that heaven is eternal, that heaven was our home before our life on earth, that heaven will be our home after our life on earth, and that heaven is where Heavenly Father and Jesus Christ, and our eternal families, will dwell forever.

Q Do Mormons believe in Jesus Christ?

Yes, Mormons have a strong belief in and commitment to the Lord Jesus Christ. They believe that He is the only begotten Son of God; that He is the Savior of all mankind; and that He is *"the way, the truth, and the life: no man cometh unto the Father, but by me"* (John 14:6).

Mormons believe that salvation is not possible without the benefit of the Atonement and Resurrection of Jesus Christ, and even then, only on the condition of faith in the Lord Jesus Christ, repentance, and Baptism by immersion for the remission of sins.

Q *Do Mormons believe in being "born again"?*

Yes, Mormons believe in being born again.

Now, there are certain fundamentalist and evangelical Christian groups that use the term *Born-Again Christian.* This is a terminology that they've claimed for their own, and they're angry when they hear Mormons referring to themselves as Christians or as born-again Christians.

However, Mormons fully believe that being born again— as explained by Jesus Christ in the New Testament (see John 3:1–13, and elsewhere)—is a reference to being baptized by water and being given the Gift of the Holy Ghost. And because Mormons strongly believe in Baptism, and claim that their Baptism is authorized by God (remember, Mormons are Baptized in the name of Jesus Christ), they consider their Baptism *is* being born again.

So, yes, Mormons say that they've been born again, by immersion in the waters of Baptism, and being brought out as a new person, having been born of the spirit. But because evangelical Christian groups, who often are hostile and anti-Mormon, use the term *Born-Again Christian,* most Mormons do not refer to themselves using that terminology.

Q
Do Mormons believe that mankind is saved by grace alone?

This is a question that differentiates many of the Christian denominations. There are those who pin all of their beliefs on the doctrine of Divine Grace. And Divine Grace (generally defined as God's help or strength, given through the bounteous mercy and love of Jesus Christ) is the doctrine that states that because no one is without sin, no one could qualify to return to heaven without the Savior's mercy and Atonement for their sins.

Many Christians believe that this grace is a free gift from the Savior to those who believe, and that all they need to do is believe in Him (or accept Him as their personal Savior), and their sins will then be washed away, and they will be saved in the eternities. They claim that good works, or repentance from misdeeds, are *not* conditions for receiving this grace, or this forgiveness from sins.

There are others, of course, who *do* believe that people's behavior matters, and that people will be judged by their deeds (their "works") in this life (see James 2:10–26). However, those who pin all their hope on the doctrine of grace say that it's an affront to God to believe that people can work out their own salvation based on their good works alone . . . and that any focus on deeds, or works, or people's behavior, is misguided. They see salvation as a gift of Jesus to those who believe on His name.

Mormons really take a different position. They are believers in both the principle of Justice (obey God's laws through your works, or you can't return to heaven), *and* the principle of Mercy (disobedience can be forgiven through sincere repentance, due to the grace of the Lord Jesus Christ, through His Atonement and sacrifice). They believe that Jesus' Resurrection is a free gift to all, but that His Atonement for their sins can only be accessed through faith in His name, sincere repentance, Baptism by one having authority, and the Holy Ghost . . . all of which provide a way for people to have their sins forgiven, if they repent.

This is the doctrine of grace in which Mormons believe. But they also believe in the doctrine of justice, which says that if someone who is a murderer, for example, comes to believe in Jesus, that he isn't automatically going to get the full benefit of Christ's mercy unto salvation unless he repents of his murdering. And therefore, Mormons believe that it is a combination of these two doctrines that is God's true plan.

The Mormon view is that no one can make it, no matter how good they are, without the gift of the grace of God. But that, within the context of that gift, the level of heaven to which people will be resurrected, will be dependent upon how righteously, honorably, and charitably they lived their lives. Mormons believe that, without grace, they would not have a chance to repent, be washed clean, or live in the eternities at all; but once that gift was given, that their personal behavior—based upon their own free agency to choose their own behavior—will be the determining factor in terms of how they will be judged, and where in heaven they will be assigned to live.

Therefore, Mormons believe that both doctrines are true: that Jesus is the only way to salvation, but that it still makes a difference how you live your life—whether you live a righteous life, a life with repentance and continuous improvement, or a life filled with iniquity, sin, and degradation . . . without any effort to repent or improve.

Q Don't Mormons believe that you can earn your way to heaven by your good works?

No. Mormons believe that without Christ's Atonement and Resurrection, and His serving as the Savior of the world, no one can get to heaven, no matter how many good works a person has done. But as explained in the previous question, within the context of the gift of grace that Jesus provided to all, Mormons believe that someone's behavior will be a factor in determining *where* in heaven he or she will be resurrected: the more righteous, the higher degree of heaven (where God the Father and Jesus Christ live); the more unrighteous, the lower degree of heaven.

Q What do Mormons think are the steps to repentance?

In general, Mormons believe that God has taught mankind to follow the following steps to repentance:

- Recognize that you've made a mistake or committed a sin of some kind.

- Feel remorse (i.e., sorrow, shame, guilt, etc.).

- Apologize to the one offended, and make amends or restitution for any possessions that were lost or destroyed. (This is why Mormons believe that murder, rape, slander, and other such sins are so serious, because it's often impossible to make restitution in these cases.)

- Seek forgiveness from the one offended, and from God, by reliance on the Atonement and sacrifice of the Lord Jesus Christ.

- Renounce your sins, change your heart, submit your will to God, and try to endure to the end, without committing the same sin again.

Q   *Do Mormons believe in having faith?*

Yes, faith in the Lord Jesus Christ is one of the key principles of the Mormon Church. In their Articles of Faith, it states:

"We believe that the first principles and ordinances of the Gospel are: first, Faith in the Lord Jesus Christ; second, Repentance; third, Baptism by immersion for the remission of sins; fourth, Laying on of hands for the gift of the Holy Ghost."

—Article 4

And the first of their Articles of Faith defines what they believe in:

"We believe in God, the Eternal Father, and in His Son, Jesus Christ, and in the Holy Ghost."

—Article 1

Further they believe the Apostle Paul's definition of faith, as follows:

"Now faith is the substance of things hoped for, the evidence of things not seen."

—Hebrews 11:1

As you can tell, faith in the existence of God, and in the Plan of Salvation—as laid out by the Savior, the Lord Jesus Christ—is central to Mormonism's view of *why* we're here, *where* we came from, and *what* lies ahead.

Q Do Mormons believe in original sin?

While most Christians and Jews interpret the concept of "original" sin to mean that all mankind would be punished for Adam and Eve's sin of disobeying God's commandment by partaking of the forbidden fruit, Mormons have a slightly different take. They believe that Adam and Eve's disobedience caused them to be cast out of the Garden of Eden (where, had they remained, they would have been immortal), and that this brought about mortality, which meant that all men would eventually die a physical death. However, Mormons do not believe that people today are being punished for Adam and Eve's transgression (unless you consider mortality to be a punishment), because their Articles of Faith state:

"We believe that men will be punished for their own sins, and not for Adam's transgression."

—Article 2

In fact, Mormons also don't believe that it was Eve's "fault" that Adam partook of the forbidden fruit. They believe that Adam and Eve were presented with two conflicting commandments, which were a part of God's plan from the beginning: 1) either obey the commandment to not eat the forbidden fruit, and remain in the Garden of Eden, where they would not be able to obey the commandment to multiply and replenish the earth (because Mormons believe that they would not be able to create children with mortal bodies while in the immortal state provided by the Garden of Eden); or 2) obey the commandment to multiply and replenish the earth, which required them to be cast out of the Garden of Eden, which could only occur if they disobeyed the commandment to not eat of the forbidden fruit.

Mormons believe that the second choice was an integral part of God's Plan of Salvation from the beginning, and that God allowed Satan to tempt the innocent Adam and Eve into taking the proscribed step, in order to begin the process of allowing the spirit children of God to be born into the mortal bodies of Adam and Eve's physical children (and their progeny), on earth.

Q *Do Mormons believe in Hell and Satan?*

Yes. Mormons are strong believers in the basic teachings of the early Christian Church. However, their understanding of Satan and hell represents a different interpretation from that of most Catholic and Protestant denominations.

Mormons believe that all things were created by God. They also believe that He created billions of spirit children, who lived with Him in heaven, and who are the spirits that He sends to be born onto this earth to gain physical bodies. Mormons believe that His firstborn child in heaven was Jesus Christ (although they believe that *Jesus* was the name God told Joseph and Mary to give him upon his birth on earth, that *Christ* [the Greek word for "Messiah"] is the "title" of his priesthood "office" in the Plan of Salvation, and that his actual premortal name in heaven was *Jehovah*).

Although the Scriptures don't specifically indicate it, it's possible that Lucifer was perhaps God's second son in heaven, and that Lucifer and Jesus (and all of us, for that matter) were brothers (and sisters), as spirit children of Heavenly Father.

Mormons believe that, long before Adam and Eve were ever born, there was a council in heaven (among all of God's children), to discuss what was needed to create an earth, in order to permit all of these spirit children to be born into physical bodies and to learn to develop Christ-like character traits. According to Mormons, these two eldest brothers, Jesus and Lucifer, presented different approaches for implementing God's Plan of Salvation.

Jesus' plan was to create an earth onto which everyone would be born, but that a *veil* would be placed between these mortals and their recollection of their prior life in heaven. They would also be given their own free agency to either choose to exercise faith in pursuing righteousness, or to choose to live their lives without faith, and without developing the Christ-like qualities that would permit them to return to live with their Heavenly Father in heaven. Furthermore, Jesus offered to willingly sacrifice Himself to serve as the needed Savior in order to provide an opportunity for repentance and forgiveness for those who believed, while giving all of the glory to God, His Father.

Mormons believe that Lucifer's plan was similar, except that he was not going to have a veil, and he was not going to allow people their free agency; rather, he would just forcibly require everyone to be obedient to all of God's commandments, while claiming all the glory for himself for having brought all of Heavenly Father's children back safely to heaven.

According to the Mormon Church, God knew (as did Jesus), that "forcing" people to be righteous, was not the same as having people "choose" for themselves to be righteous . . . even if they were only basing their decisions on faith, and in the face of considerable efforts by non-believers to persuade them otherwise. Because He knew that Jesus' plan was based on truth and God's laws, Mormons believe that God chose Jesus' plan, and that Lucifer responded in anger, which resulted in his being cast out of heaven (see Isaiah 14:12–23; Luke 10:18; and Revelation 12:1–17) . . . along with one-third of the spirit children of God (Revelation 12:4), who had sided with Lucifer during this "war in heaven" (Revelation 12:7) . . . never to have the opportunity to be born onto the earth and receive physical bodies, thus eternally denying them access back to their original home in heaven. (In *Les Miserables*, Victor

Hugo makes extensive references to this dismissal of Lucifer from heaven.)

Mormons believe that, from that day forth, Lucifer has been referred to as Satan, or the devil. They believe that neither Satan nor any of his followers will be born into bodies on this earth . . . but are here on earth in spirit form, and are trying to keep as many people as possible from following the straight and narrow path that leads to salvation. Mormons view Satan and his followers, hidden though they may be, as the primary force on the earth that is attempting to dissuade people from exercising faith in Jesus Christ, from choosing righteousness, from joining the true Church, and from obeying the commandments. They believe that he exerts a powerful influence on all the people who have been born into the world, who, because the veil has been drawn, are exposed and vulnerable to the buffetings, trials, and tribulations that Satan is putting them through.

In this regard, Mormons believe that Satan was once a beloved son of God, but who, through disobedience, was forever cast out, and is now (rather successfully) trying to keep as many people as possible from following Jesus' teachings.

This is how Mormons get their view of hell as well. Mormons do not see hell as literally a bottomless pit where the wicked will dwell with "fire and brimstone," but rather they see hell as a lower level of heaven, where those people who fail to qualify for the higher levels of heaven will be sent because of their own behavior, and their own choice not to follow the Lord Jesus Christ. To them it will be a hell, because they will realize that they could have qualified for a higher degree of heaven, but through their own poor choices and lack of faith, failed to do so.

Now, of course, there are those extremely wicked and evil people—the Hitlers and Stalins of the world—who will be sent to what Mormons refer to as Outer Darkness, which is outside the realm of heaven, and is where there will be "weeping and wailing and gnashing of teeth," and where they'll suffer in torment, with Satan and his followers, eternally.

Mormons have great faith that God the Father loves all of His children, and wants them to come home safely to Him, where He will reward them with a life in heaven that is much more wonderful than anything possible on earth. But Mormons contend that the people who don't get to the highest level of heaven, after they die and are resurrected, will be shamefully disappointed, and will consider it a form of hell to have failed—through pride, disobedience, or some other sin or misdeed—to qualify to live with Heavenly Father and Jesus . . . even though they'll still be blessed by living in a part of heaven that is more wonderful and joyful than anything on earth.

Q

Do Mormons think that all those who haven't even heard the Gospel of Jesus Christ will still go to Hell, as do some other churches?

No. Mormons believe that people who have lived on the earth, but who have never heard about Jesus Christ and have never been taught the Gospel, are not automatically going to hell. Mormons believe that they'll have the same opportunities that all of Heavenly Father's children have.

Their view is that God is a just God. He loves His children, and would not deny those who happen to be born in Africa four thousand years ago, for example, to go to hell through no fault of their own; whereas those who have been born in America and have had the opportunity to hear the Gospel might have the chance for eternal salvation. Mormons think that this is not what a loving father would do. And therefore, they believe that God has provided a way for *all* of His children who have ever lived, to return home to heaven, to be with Him again.

In fact, because Jesus teaches that *everyone* must be baptized, Mormons believe that God has provided a wonderful way for those who've died without ever having heard the Gospel to still receive the ordinance of Baptism. Mormons perform Baptisms for the Dead in their temples. Mormons believe that, once baptized, the living spirits of those people who have died will then be taught the Gospel in paradise (a place in the afterlife, where the spirits of people who have died await resurrection and final judgment); and that, at the end of the Millennium—the thousand-year reign of the Lord Jesus Christ on earth—those people will also have the opportunity to gain exaltation and eternal life in heaven.

Mormons also believe that those who are under the age of eight, and have therefore never had the chance to be baptized . . . will automatically go to heaven, because they are not accountable for their behavior in this life, nor for whether or not their parents ever introduced them to the Gospel of Jesus Christ. Therefore, according to Mormons, rather than being penalized for not having been able to hear the Gospel or live their lives to the fullest, those who have died prior to the age of eight are being rewarded for their goodness and their sacrifice by being given automatic entrance into the Celestial Kingdom of heaven.

Q What do Mormons believe about the Second Coming?

The Second Coming refers to a Christian doctrine that asserts that Jesus Christ will return to earth a second time (the first time being His birth into mortal life, continuing through His Crucifixion on the Cross). Mormons fully embrace this doctrine. They believe that Jesus Christ will return in glory to the earth . . . to reign over His people for a thousand years. They believe that His Second Coming will follow periods of horrible wars and bloodshed, and that the wicked will be destroyed prior to His return.

Q *Do Mormons believe in the rapture?*

This is an interesting question, but it's only pertinent to a small group of people, because most people (including most Christians) have never heard of the *rapture*. The rapture is a term used by evangelical Christian groups to refer to those righteous members of Christ's Church who, upon Christ's Second Coming, will be physically "caught up . . . in the air" to meet Him as He returns to earth from heaven at His Second Coming.

The term *rapture* is generally used only by these certain evangelical Christian groups; however, the New Testament (see 1 Thessalonians 4:17) does refer to those righteous believers who will rise to meet the Resurrected Savior when He returns in glory at the Second Coming. Mormons believe in this doctrine (although they don't use the term *rapture*). They believe that the righteous will rise at Christ's Second Coming.

As stated elsewhere, Mormons believe that God wants, hopes for, and is providing an opportunity for all of His children to repent, to become Christ-like, and to return to Him. And so Mormons do not dwell on this concept of what will happen to those people who are still alive as Jesus' Second Coming approaches; rather, they focus their attentions on each and every one of themselves. They ask: "Am I personally living righteously enough to be found worthy to be caught up in the air during Christ's Second Coming?"

To Mormons, the rapture is only a matter of concern if we're still alive during Christ's Second Coming. If we die before then, Mormons believe that if they're righteous they'll be sent to paradise; and if they're unrighteous, they'll be sent to spirit prison. But should they be alive on the earth at the Second Coming, they hope to be righteous enough to be caught up with Him when Christ comes.

Q Do Mormons believe in the Millennium?

Yes, Mormons believe that Jesus' Second Coming will bring about a thousand-year reign of the Lord Jesus Christ on the earth. They believe that after the wicked are destroyed, Satan will be "bound" for these thousand years, thus allowing for a thousand years of righteousness to occur. They also believe that there will be those who continue to give birth to children, to raise families, and to live their lives during this time when Jesus Himself is at the head of His Church and reigns in glory over the whole earth for these thousand years.

Q *Do Mormons believe in the Resurrection?*

Yes, Mormons are strong believers that Jesus Christ is the only begotten Son of God the Father; that He took upon Himself the sins of all mankind, and suffered and atoned for them in the Garden of Gethsemane; that He willingly gave up His life on the Cross; that He raised His own body from the dead after three days; that He was the first fruits of the Resurrection; and that, through His gift, all mankind will be resurrected after they die . . . which will reunite their eternal spirits with the physical bodies that they had when they lived on earth. Mormons believe the Apostle Paul when he stated:

"For as in Adam all die, even so in Christ shall all be made alive."

—1 Corinthians 15:22

Mormons have complete faith that there is life after death. And because of this belief, they have no fear of death . . . just a fear that they may not be worthy or righteous enough to qualify for the highest, or Celestial Kingdom of heaven.

Q

Do Mormons practice Baptism? And if so, is it by sprinkling or immersion?

Mormons have always believed in the ordinance of Baptism. They believe that Baptism—performed by one in authority, in the name of Jesus Christ, for the remission of sins (Acts 2:38)—has always been one of the saving ordinances of the Gospel of Jesus Christ; and that Jesus Himself showed how important it was . . . by having John the Baptist baptize Him in the River Jordan.

All members of the Mormon Church are baptized, whether they grow up in the Church or are converted to the Church at a later age. Mormons believe that, as John the Baptist taught, and as Jesus confirmed, all people need to repent and be baptized, in order to return to live with their Father in heaven.

Mormons practice Baptism by immersion, as Jesus and John the Baptist taught in the New Testament. A typical Mormon Baptismal ceremony has members of the local congregation meet, either in a ward chapel building (where there is an actual baptismal font) or at an area swimming pool, river, or other suitable location, where one of the elders of the priesthood, who has the authority from God to perform such an ordinance, takes the baptized person by the arm, and speaks the following Baptismal words, after having stated the name of the person being baptized:

"Having been commissioned of Jesus Christ, I baptize you in the name of the Father, and of the Son, and of the Holy Ghost. Amen."

—Doctrine & Covenants 20:73

The priesthood holder then (under the watchful eyes of two witnesses to make sure that the immersion is complete) gently lowers the person into the water, and immediately brings him or her back up out of the water, thus completing the Baptism.

Mormons believe that Baptism is the "strait and narrow gate" through which people join Christ's Church and receive a remission (cleansing and forgiveness) of their sins. They believe that those who've been baptized, and have truly repented of their prior sins, will not only have those sins forgiven, but that God will also "forget" them . . . and that they will be able to begin life as a new person, "born again" because of the great mercy and grace of God the Father, and His Son, Jesus Christ.

For Mormons, the companion ordinance to Baptism is the bestowal of The Gift of the Holy Ghost through the laying on of hands by those in authority, and their confirming the newly baptized person a member of The Church of Jesus Christ of Latter-day Saints. This is done either shortly after the Baptism, or at the next Sunday worship service . . . whereby priesthood holders place their hands on the head of the person being confirmed, and, after stating the authority by which the ordinance is being performed—and that it's being done "in the name of Jesus Christ"—they give The Gift of the Holy Ghost to the newly baptized person, and confirm him or her a member of the Church. Before completing the ordinance, they will also frequently add other words of blessing and counsel, as directed by the spirit.

In exactly this same fashion, both children of Mormon families (once they've reached the age of eight), and all converts to the Church (of all ages, as long as they're at least eight), are baptized. Of course, there are people who convert to the Mormon Church from other faiths, who've already been baptized by those other churches. While respecting the tradition of those other churches, Mormons believe that all people need to be baptized by someone who has the proper authority to baptize in the name of Jesus Christ, and so Mormons will baptize all converts anew by a holder of the Melchizedek Priesthood.

Q At what age do Mormons baptize children?

Mormon children are baptized no younger than eight years old. This is because Mormons believe that, prior to that age, children are not accountable for their own actions or decisions, and are, therefore, not capable of committing true sin. Mormons believe that, should children die before they turn eight years old, they will automatically return to the Celestial Kingdom of heaven to live eternally with God the Father without the stains of sin, and without needing the repentance or cleansing that comes with Baptism. Mormons assert that such young children are not responsible for their mistakes and weaknesses, and have not yet learned the principles of the Gospel or of repentance, and therefore need not be baptized.

Q *What's the deal about Mormons baptizing people after they've died? Do they really do this?*

It's true that Mormons perform Baptisms for the Dead in their temples. But to clear up any possible confusion, Mormons don't baptize dead bodies. They baptize living people (members of the Mormon Church who volunteer for this service), who stand in as proxies for those people who have died. They believe that such Baptisms for the Dead are a part of God's merciful Plan of Salvation, by which He has provided a way for *all* of His children to receive the required ordinance of Baptism . . . even if they lived on earth during a time when there were no priesthood holders authorized to perform Baptisms, or if they lived in a nation that had never heard of Jesus Christ.

They believe Jesus when he said: *"Except a man be born of water and of the spirit, he cannot enter into the kingdom of God"* (John 3:5); and *"He that believeth and is baptized shall be saved; but he that believeth not shall be damned"* (Mark 16:16). Mormons take this to mean that, in order to gain salvation, *all* must be baptized . . . but that it wouldn't be just or fair if some had the opportunity to be baptized, while others did not. And therefore they believe that God authorized Baptisms for the Dead as a part of His Plan of Salvation for all of His children. While most Christians ignore the following words of the Apostle Paul, or merely see them as referring to some unknown and unimportant Jewish rite, Mormons site them as supportive of their belief:

"Else what shall they do which are baptized for the dead, if the dead rise not at all? why are they then baptized for the dead?"

—1 Corinthians 15:29

One of the reasons Mormons build temples is so that they can perform such Baptisms. And one of the reasons why they spend so much time and energy on gathering genealogical records, is so that they can identify everyone who has ever lived on the earth, so that they can all be baptized.

While some groups seem offended that Mormons are baptizing people of other faiths (in fact, many old genealogical records don't record religious preferences, anyway), Mormons are quick to add that they're just doing this as a service of love; that the deceased person is under no obligation to accept the validity of the Baptism or to join the Mormon Church in heaven, should he or she not want to. Frankly, they are somewhat baffled at why non-Mormons would care what Mormons do in their temples, if they don't believe Mormon doctrines are valid and don't believe that the Mormon Church is Jesus' true Church.

Mormons merely contend that should these deceased people decide to hear the Gospel in heaven, and join the Church, then they will already have had the required ordinances performed for them, by proxy (in the same way that Christ performed a proxy sacrifice—through His Atonement and Crucifixion—so that all mankind may have the opportunity to repent and be cleansed from sin).

Mormons are apparently the only ones performing such Baptisms for the Dead; however, they see this practice as an indication of both the justice and mercy of a loving God. While most faiths see non-members of their own faith as doomed to some form of hell . . . Mormons believe that a just God would not permit *some* of His children to be saved, while others are damned just because they happened to be born in different circumstances, in different times, and to parents of different faiths.

Q *Do Mormons really believe that the wedding ceremonies held in their temples allow husbands and wives to stay married even after they've died, and not just "until death do us part"?*

Yes. While nearly all wedding ceremonies performed by clergy of other faiths use the words "until death do you part," Mormon temple wedding ceremonies use the words ". . . for time and all eternity."

As stated in their 1995 Proclamation to the World, Mormons believe that "marriage between a man and a woman is ordained of God and that the family is central to the Creator's plan for the eternal destiny of His children." They believe that God wants *all* of His children to marry happily, raise families, and bring them back home together—as intact family units—to live with Him in heaven, throughout the eternities.

For Mormons, the opportunity to be able to live together as a family, throughout the eternities of heaven, is a powerful motivator . . . and is one of the primary reasons why Mormons are so focused on living worthy enough to qualify to go to the temple.

17 MORMON RELIGIOUS PRACTICES: PRAYER, WORSHIP SERVICES, SACRAMENT/ COMMUNION, FASTING, TITHE-PAYING, BAPTISM, EXCOMMUNICATION, CROSSES, CONGREGATIONAL STRUCTURE, HOLIDAYS, AND SO ON

Q *Do Mormons pray?*

Yes, Mormons pray, both silently to themselves and publicly in front of groups. They begin and end their worship services with prayer; they begin and end their various classes and administrative meetings with prayer; they pray for those who are sick or afflicted; and they're taught to pray often. In fact, from a very early age, Mormon children are taught to pray every morning after they get up, every evening before they go to bed, and before each meal . . . and to thank Heavenly Father often for their many blessings at His hand.

Mormon Church doctrine is to pray to God the Father in the name of Jesus Christ. Generally, Mormons see praying as holding a sacred conversation with their Heavenly Father. They typically begin by saying: "Dear Heavenly Father." They then proceed to thank Him for all of the blessings they've received (both generally and specifically), and then ask Him for help—with decisions they might be facing, trials they might be going through, or behaviors they might be trying to improve—for forgiveness of their weaknesses and missteps, and for blessings that they're in need of.

Mormons are then taught to close each prayer "... in the name of Jesus Christ, Amen," as it is their belief—because God sent Jesus Christ to be the great intercessor between His disobedient, sinful, and ungrateful children on earth and their merciful, loving, and perfect Father who is in heaven—that He has commanded them to invoke Christ's holy name in all of their communications with Him.

Except for the prayers offered as a part of certain ordinances—such as Baptism, partaking of the Sacrament, and in certain other ordinances that are performed in Mormon temples—almost all other prayers given by Mormons are unrehearsed and from the heart ... usually spoken quietly, in a serene, reverent, and very personal manner. Mormons pray aloud, they pray in secret, and they say grace over their meals. And in addition to each person's daily personal prayers, many Mormons have both morning and evening family prayers together.

Q Do Mormons say the Lord's Prayer?

Yes, Mormons know and say the Lord's Prayer, as found in the Bible (Matthew 6:9–13). They also believe that, after His Resurrection (and the visit that Mormons claim that He made to the American continent, as recorded in the Book of Mormon), Jesus taught this prayer to His followers there, as well.

However, Mormons generally do not recite the Lord's Prayer in unison, as many Christian denominations do, because it's their belief that Jesus used the Lord's Prayer to teach His followers *how* to construct a prayer . . . not that He wanted them to continually repeat a rote prayer, that didn't come from the heart, or that didn't address the specific concerns that each person might have.

Q What goes on in a Mormon worship service? Are there sermons and hymns?

Mormon worship services are held every Sunday, and usually last for three hours. Their primary worship service, which they call their Sacrament meeting, occurs during the first hour and ten minutes. Because there are no paid ministers, there's no one person who's designated to give a sermon each week. In fact, Mormons don't generally use the term *sermon* at all; instead, they have members who give "talks" in their Sacrament meetings.

The local bishop will occasionally give a talk, as will his two counselors in the bishopric, but all members of the local congregation will rotate giving talks on Gospel topics throughout the year, by invitation of the bishop. Most such talks will vary from five to fifteen minutes in length . . . and a typical worship service might have two to four such talks, after the Sacrament of the Lord's Supper is blessed and passed to the congregation.

Most Mormon Sacrament meetings follow this pattern: an opening hymn is sung; an opening prayer is given; local Church business is conducted; the bread and water of the Sacrament is blessed and passed to the congregation; several speakers (often youth speakers) give their brief talks; a rest hymn is then sung; one or two other speakers (usually adult members of the ward) give their brief talks; and then there is a closing hymn, followed by a closing prayer. This is what constitutes a typical Mormon worship service.

The next fifty minutes or so represents the Sunday School portion of a Mormon Church service . . . where there are a number of separate classes for each different age group. Gospel Doctrine is the principal class for adults, but there are other Sunday School classes for twelve- through seventeen-year-olds, Primary classes for children under twelve, and a nursery for those under three.

The third hour is typically used for additional Sunday lessons . . . with the men going to their priesthood meetings, where they teach each other principles of the Gospel; the women going to their Relief Society meetings, where they teach each other principles of the Gospel; the teenage youth going to their various Young Men's and Young Women's Organization meetings; and the younger children continuing with their Primary activities, as carried over from the Sunday School period.

Depending upon the talents and skills that exist within each congregation, and on the size of the building, there is usually a piano and/or a portable organ in the chapel; and, if there's sufficient interest, there's usually a ward choir. Mormon choir members do not wear special choir robes, but merely come to the front of the chapel to sing hymns that they've prepared and rehearsed.

The Mormon hymn book is very similar to most Protestant hymnals, with perhaps half of the hymns being the same ones that appear in many other Christian denominational hymn books—such as *All Creatures of Our God and King,* *A Mighty Fortress Is Our God,* *God of Our Fathers, Whose Almighty Hand,* *How Great Thou Art,* *I Need Thee Every Hour,* *Nearer, My God, to Thee,* *Rock of Ages,* *Sweet Hour of Prayer,* *Christ the Lord Is Risen Today,* *Silent Night,* *Praise God, from Whom All Blessings Flow,* *How Gentle God's Commands,* *Jesus, the Very Thought of Thee,* among others—and the other half being hymns that have been written by Mormon composers from the 1830s through the present time . . . including the world-famous pioneer hymn, written during the Mormon exodus to Utah: *Come, Come, Ye Saints.*

Q *Do Mormons take Communion?*

Yes. Mormons take Communion once a week during their Sunday Sacrament meeting worship services. Their term for Communion (some denominations call it the Sacrament of the Last Supper of Our Lord, or the Holy Eucharist), is Partaking of the Sacrament . . . and they even refer to their principal Sunday worship service as their Sacrament meeting.

During this meeting, the sacramental bread and water are blessed and passed to the congregation in remembrance of the body and blood of the Lord Jesus Christ. Here's the prayer that Mormon priesthood holders speak over the broken bread:

> *"O God, the Eternal Father, we ask thee in the name of thy Son, Jesus Christ, to bless and sanctify this bread to the souls of all those who partake of it, that they may eat in remembrance of the body of thy Son, and witness unto thee, O God, the Eternal Father, that they are willing to take upon them the name of thy Son, and always remember him and keep his commandments which he has given them; that they may always have his Spirit to be with them. Amen."*
>
> —Doctrine & Covenants 20:77

And here's the prayer that Mormon priesthood holders speak over the water:

> *"O God, the Eternal Father, we ask thee in the name of thy Son, Jesus Christ, to bless and sanctify this water to the souls of all those who drink of it, that they may do it*

in remembrance of the blood of thy Son, which was shed
for them; that they may witness unto thee, O God, the
Eternal Father, that they do always remember him, that
they may have his Spirit to be with them. Amen."

—Doctrine & Covenants 20:79

As taught in the New Testament, Mormons believe that Jesus introduced the Sacrament of the Last Supper to his disciples, the Apostles, just prior to his betrayal, trial, and Crucifixion . . . with the commandment that the believing faithful should continue to partake of the Sacrament in remembrance of His life, His Atonement and sacrifice on the Cross for all mankind, His Resurrection, and His mercy and grace . . . which Mormons believe He extends unto all who follow Him in righteousness.

Originally, Mormons broke bread and drank wine for their Sacrament. But when Joseph Smith claimed to have received the revelation called The Word of Wisdom—and Mormons were counseled to not drink alcohol of any kind—the prophet and other Church leaders prayed for guidance, and were told to substitute water, instead of wine, for the Sacrament service . . . for both were merely symbolic of the blood of Jesus Christ, and that water was fully acceptable in the eyes of God. Therefore, Mormon congregations simply use bread and water in their Sacrament services.

Q Do Mormons fast?

Yes. In fact, Mormons typically fast once a month, usually on the first Sunday of each month. On that day, Mormons fast by not partaking of any food or drink (including not drinking any water), for at least two meals, and often for twenty-four hours, prior to the Sunday services, at which time they break their fast by partaking of the sacramental bread and water.

Mormons fast as a way of showing God that they're grateful for the many blessings they've been given, that they're serious about the prayers they're offering, that they're obedient to His admonition to fast and pray often, and that they're willing to sacrifice their own comfort and ease— through fasting—as a part of their worship of Him.

As an integral part of each monthly Fast and Testimony day, every family is encouraged to make a donation to the Church, representing the amount of money that their family would have spent on the meals they would have eaten that day had they not been fasting. All such donations make up the Fast Offering Fund, which is used to provide immediate financial or other support to those families who are in need of emergency help of one kind or another—due to unexpected hardship or difficulty—as part of the Mormon welfare services program.

Because each local congregation collects Fast Offering funds monthly, they then have a supply of emergency funds available to help those who are out of work, laid up, or facing some other unexpected crisis. Any unused surplus from these funds is then combined with those of other local congregations and retained at the stake level to provide additional funds should one local congregation need more for emergency welfare than it takes in during any given month.

The same is true at the churchwide level. If a stake ever has surplus Fast Offering funds, they're sent to Church headquarters, where all such monies are accumulated for distribution to those people who are facing emergencies like earthquakes, floods, typhoons, etc. throughout the world . . . such as in Kosovo, Somalia, Bosnia, Africa, China, North Korea, or wherever the current needs are the greatest.

Typically, therefore, most Mormons fast about twelve times a year. And although this practice is not widely known by non-Mormons (and certainly not something Mormons do in order to get praise), it represents another sign of Mormons' desire to be obedient to the commandments of God. Furthermore, aside from these planned fasts, many Mormons fast and pray privately, for special concerns or family illnesses.

Q *Mormons use the word "testimony" a lot. What do they mean when they talk about "bearing their testimony"?*

To Mormons, a *testimony* is each individual's assertion that he or she believes certain things to be true. Just as witnesses give their testimony in court about what they've seen or heard and believe to be true, Mormons give their testimony in church about what they've experienced and believe to be true . . . as it pertains to their faith in the Lord Jesus Christ and His Church.

Testimony bearing is important to Mormons. So much so, that they've even designated one of their monthly Sunday Sacrament meetings as Fast and Testimony day. The worship service on Fast and Testimony day represents a time when individual members of the congregation can get up and bear their testimonies of the divinity of the Lord Jesus Christ. Often these are very spiritual meetings and represent a high point in Mormon worship services.

And should you ever be curious about what Mormons might say when they bear their testimonies, just ask the next Mormon missionary you run into. He or she will gladly bear his or her testimony for you, right there on the spot.

Is it true that Mormons actually have to be interviewed by their minister every year? And he asks them if they believe in Jesus Christ, if they treat their family well, and if they don't smoke or drink, and all those things?

Yes, in order to be allowed to enter the temple, Mormons have to receive a "permission slip" from their bishop, which is called a *temple recommend*. That recommend form is the result of an interview between a bishop and a member, which is typically held annually, and which covers such basic questions as: Do you believe in God? Do you believe that Jesus Christ is your Savior? Do you believe that the president of the Church is a true prophet of Jesus Christ, and is the leader of His Church and priesthood on the earth? Are you honest in all your dealings with your fellow men? Do you obey The Word of Wisdom by not smoking, by not drinking alcohol, and by not drinking tea or coffee? Are you a good husband and father, or wife and mother? Do you treat your children well? . . . and other similar kinds of questions.

This is a fascinating process that Mormons go through. In most churches, this level of insightful self-examination does not involve a face-to-face conversation with the minister. But in the Mormon Church, this process provides a confidential opportunity for Mormons to reaffirm their basic core beliefs once a year, and to reevaluate their own progress in attempting to become better people . . . all during a private conversation with their bishop, and separately with their stake president.

Once they have a signed temple recommend form, they then have the needed authorization to enter the temple, and perform the sacred temple ordinances that Mormons feel are so important for themselves and their deceased ancestors.

Q Is it true that Mormons pay a full 10 percent tithe on all their income?

Yes. Active Mormons who want to pass the annual inquiry into whether they are worthy to attend their temple do pay a full 10 percent tithe on all their income—and that's on their gross income, not their net after-tax income. Mormons believe that tithing is a commandment of God. And while there are some Mormons who, for one reason or another, do not pay a full 10 percent and are not kicked out of the Church, neither are they permitted to attend the temple until they're able to acknowledge that they've become full tithe-payers again.

In recognition for all the blessings and gifts, mercy and divine assistance that come from God, Mormons believe that He merely asks that His children return *to* Him one-tenth of what they get *from* Him. Their view is that if He provides everything, then our being asked to tithe is not our having to give away 10 percent of what is *ours*, but rather that we get to keep 90 percent of what is *His*. Mormons believe that the Old Testament prophets taught this principle, and that even Abraham had to pay tithes . . . and paid his tithes to Melchizedek, who was his Church leader at the time (see Hebrews 7:1–5).

While many churches pass an offering plate at each service and collect weekly donations and pledges in that form, Mormons do not ever pass an offering plate. Mormons either hand their tithing payments or checks directly to their local bishop, or mail them in as they receive their paychecks. Many Mormons have a strong testimony of the principle of tithing. They believe that if they are faithful in their paying of tithes, God will bless them for their obedience . . . with better-paying jobs, with freedom from financial crises, and with special help when tough times do come.

200

Q *Do Mormons christen their babies?*

Although they don't use the term *christening,* soon after the birth of their children, most Mormon fathers (or other close relative or friend, if the father doesn't hold the priesthood in the Mormon Church) give their infant children a special priesthood blessing, during which they announce the name that is being given to the newly born son or daughter of God, and pronounce blessings upon the baby, as moved upon by the spirit.

This blessing usually takes place during a Sacrament meeting, and is usually attended by as many relatives and friends as can arrange their schedules to be in attendance . . . with many often coming from hundreds or thousands of miles away.

Q What do Mormons do about members of their Church who commit sins?

Mormons believe that *all* people are Heavenly Father's children, and are under an obligation to learn to follow Jesus Christ and live His Gospel. In this regard, they don't see themselves as any different from non-members of their church.

They believe that everyone who commits transgressions needs to repent of their transgressions, and needs to seek forgiveness . . . both from the person against whom the transgression was made, and from God. To Mormons, the process of repentance is the one that Jesus Christ Himself taught . . . since they see Him as the author of repentance, through His atoning sacrifice. They see the process of repentance as including these steps: acknowledging that you've made a mistake; having godly sorrow for it; making restitution to the one offended; seeking forgiveness; and covenanting with Heavenly Father to not commit that transgression again.

Mormons believe, as long as transgressors are sincere and righteous in their efforts to repent, that Jesus Christ will forgive them, wash away their "uncleanness" (through His atoning blood), and ultimately forget that they ever sinned. In this way, Mormons believe that people will be able to continue with their lives, either until they die or until they commit another sin. They see this sometimes difficult process of repentance as a wonderful and merciful part of Heavenly Father's Plan of Salvation . . . and the only way by which people can have their sins forgiven, and thereby be made clean enough to return to live with God in heaven.

Mormons who commit serious transgressions (such as spousal or child abuse, sexual abuse, adultery, criminal felonies, and so on) can be excommunicated from the Church, and must then be rebaptized, after a sufficient amount of time has gone by . . . and with the broken heart and contrite spirit that Jesus expects of those who are willing to be baptized in His name, for the remission of their sins. Mormons that commit transgressions that do not require excommunication can be "disfellowshipped," or placed on other levels of "probation" within the Church . . . or might just be counseled on a private, confidential basis by their bishop . . . to work on repenting and improving their lives. As with most people, Mormons believe that they each have weaknesses, occasionally behave poorly, disappoint their family and others, and commit mistakes and transgressions (both small and large) daily. Therefore they are daily seeking forgiveness from Heavenly Father in their own private and personal prayers.

Q What's up with the special underwear that I hear Mormons wear?

As Jews wear yarmulkes, and other religions have certain other clothing items that are sacred to their faith, Mormons who have qualified to go to their temples and have there received sacred ordinances for themselves, are allowed to wear a special white undergarment (similar to long underwear), to remind them of the sacred covenants that they've made in the temple with God and to provide them with a protection against the influence of the adversary. These covenants are sacred to Mormons, and are not discussed openly . . . and their temple garments are not shown publicly.

These temple garments have deep significance to Mormons, and most members of the Mormon Church are generally surprised and dismayed that others who claim to be Christians would mock their sacred ordinances. If others don't share their beliefs, Mormons have no opposition to their having the freedom to choose what faith they believe in, what church they belong to, and what beliefs they have. But as Mormons don't mock the use of the cross by Protestants, the use of the crucifix by Catholics, or the use of the yarmulke by Jews . . . they're baffled that those same people would mock Mormons for the components of their religion that are sacred and important to them.

As you run into Mormons throughout your business, school, and neighborhood interactions, you'll generally find that adult Mormons don't wear shorts, and don't wear sleeveless tops, spaghetti straps, or bare-midriff clothing . . . and that's primarily because they believe that the special temple garments that God has asked them to wear (among other benefits), establishes a standard of modesty that defines what outward clothing they can wear. They believe that God wants His sons and daughters to be more modest, and to not wear revealing or otherwise immodest clothing.

As a casual observer of people (and aren't we all?), you'll generally find that Mormons dress a little more modestly than the general public. You'll also realize why most non-Mormons are totally unaware that Mormons wear special temple garments at all. Just remember that they do so to remind them of the covenants that they've made in the temple with God the Father and Jesus Christ.

Q

If they claim to be Christian, why don't Mormon Churches have Crosses on them?

Although many people have never even noticed the fact that Mormon Church buildings have no crosses on them, those few Christian denominations that are openly hostile to Mormonism are quick to say: "How can Mormons be Christian if they don't even display the Christian cross?"

While it's true that Mormon chapels often have steeples . . . there are no traditional Christian crosses anywhere to be found. In its simplest terms, Mormons feel that the cross represents a focus on the *crucified* Lord rather than a focus on the *resurrected* Lord, and because they've been taught not to use icons or graven images, Mormons don't use any icons representing their faith in their chapel buildings or temples.

However, they certainly recognize the cross as a powerful Christian symbol, and believe all of the Biblical references to "bearing one's cross" (or trials), and revere the sacrifice and voluntary death that the Lord Jesus Christ suffered on the Cross for all of mankind. And Mormons are certainly not averse to those who do use the cross as a representation of their Christian faith, and honor those who, like themselves, are trying to live Christ-like lives.

While it is not against any rules for Mormons to wear crosses, most Mormons do not wear necklaces or earrings that incorporate the symbol of the cross, because those symbols are often worn by those evangelical Christian denominations that are hostile toward the Mormon version of Christianity.

Q *But if Mormons don't use symbols such as the Cross, then why do they have a golden statue of someone on the top of most of their temples?*

This is a fair question, especially once one realizes that the statue is *not* of Jesus Christ.

The statue on the top of the spire of most Mormon temples represents the Angel Moroni who, when he lived on earth, was the prophet who buried the record of his people (the source of the Book of Mormon), in about 400 A.D. After he died, Mormons believe that it was this same Moroni who appeared to Joseph Smith in 1824 (in angelic form), and led Joseph to where he had buried the records. This enabled young Joseph to translate the records—under the divine inspiration of God—into English, and publish the Book of Mormon . . . to help provide the doctrinal clarification needed by God to restore the priesthood and the original Church of Jesus Christ, which Mormons call The Church of Jesus Christ of Latter-day Saints.

The statue of the Angel Moroni, therefore, does not represent a God that Mormons worship . . . rather it merely commemorates the sounding of the "trump" by a prophet of God, which announced the restoration of the Gospel of Jesus Christ to the earth . . . after about seventeen hundred years of apostasy.

Q   *How large are most Mormon congregations?*

Mormons call their local congregations *wards,* and each ward is given a name . . . such as the New York City Third Ward (of The Church of Jesus Christ of Latter-day Saints), or the Houston Second Ward, or the Franklin Ward (in northern Virginia). And, unlike many other churches, in which a local minister can establish a congregation that includes several thousand members, Mormon wards are organized strictly on the basis of geographic boundaries and size of membership. Every place on earth is (at least theoretically) included in some existing ward boundary.

Typically, once a local ward reaches a membership of around five hundred people, it is divided into two wards, along some easily explained geographic boundary. In this way, most Mormon congregations are made up of between two hundred and four hundred members, all of whom live in relatively close proximity to one another. Each ward, therefore, usually has about fifty to one hundred fifty families, most of which have both a mother and a father, and several children. In remote areas, where members of the Church live far apart, there are occasionally small wards that might have as few as ten to twenty people (or up to one hundred fifty or so), and those are usually called *branches* of the Church.

Typically, a geographic grouping of five to ten wards constitutes what Mormons call a *stake* (or what others might call a diocese or parish). Most stakes have between two thousand to four thousand members, and there are thousands of stakes around the world, making up the total membership of the Mormon Church . . . which is currently approaching 12 million members worldwide. It's often surprising to many, that more than half of those members live outside of the United States . . . in more than one hundred sixty countries throughout the world. While all of these members have their membership records maintained by their local ward or branch, they are all members of The (worldwide) Church of Jesus Christ of Latter-day Saints.

Q   *Are Mormons allowed to visit other churches?*

Of course. The Mormon faith is a strong advocate of free agency, and all members of the Church are free to act on their own beliefs, and to decide how to live their lives. And therefore Mormons are fully free to attend any church they would like to . . . to visit those churches, to join with their family members and neighbors who belong to those churches, to sing in their services, and to enjoy the spirit that is attendant in churches of all faiths. There is no prohibition of any kind for Mormons attending other churches.

Mormons, however, would typically not consider *joining* another church, unless they had decided to relinquish their membership in The Church of Jesus Christ of Latter-day Saints. While recognizing that many other local churches might not have a national denominational affiliation (or a worldwide organizational structure), and therefore membership in those local churches might be considered a less formal affiliation . . . for Mormons, membership in their Church is quite a formal and seriously considered affiliation. And therefore, while fully free to *visit* other churches, it's not likely that any active Mormon would consider *joining* another church.

Q *Can non-Mormons visit Mormon Churches?*

Of course. Mormon worship services are open to the public . . . and most Mormons would love to have their friends and neighbors, business associates and classmates, join them at Church. Sunday worship services usually last three hours, broken down into three sections: Sacrament meeting, Sunday School, and separate third-hour classes for both men and women. There are also once-a-week activity nights for teenagers, which are also open to visitors.

Visitors at such services would not be expected to make any donations (Mormons don't ever pass an offering plate, anyway), they wouldn't be asked to speak or pray in front of the group (other than maybe to introduce themselves in Sunday School), and they would be under no obligation to ever visit again. But they'd be welcome to partake of the Sacrament when it was passed (if they'd like to), and they'd be free to join in singing the hymns along with the congregation, if they so choose. Should you be considering visiting a Mormon Church, expect that the Church members will probably be wearing traditional "Sunday best" clothing—modest dresses or skirts and blouses for the women, and shirts and ties for the men—but there would be no special expectation for non-Mormon visitors. In general, they'd just be glad you came.

Q   *Do Mormons celebrate Christmas?*

Absolutely. As Christians, Mormons love to celebrate Christmas. They revere the story of Christ's birth to Mary and Joseph in the stable in Bethlehem; and their December Sacrament meetings ring out with all the traditional Christmas carols that are known throughout the world.

And as a family-centered people, Mormons also love to look forward to the Christmas season with all the excitement in the air . . . school vacations, Santa Claus, getting out and carefully displaying the family crêche or nativity scene, all the Christmas decorations and lights, trimming the Christmas tree, having Grandma and Grandpa come to visit, hanging the stockings by the mantle, reading *Twas the Night Before Christmas* and Luke's account of Jesus' birth in the New Testament, opening gifts, visiting nursing homes . . . and everything else that makes the Christmas season so special for most families. As you can see . . . Mormons *love* Christmas!

Q *Do Mormons celebrate Easter?*

Of course. Easter is perhaps the most sacred holiday of all for Mormons. As Christians, they believe—had it not been for Jesus' Atonement, sacrifice, and Resurrection on Easter—that all mankind would be permanently kept from being able to return home to heaven . . . to live with God the Father and His son Jesus Christ. They believe that "no unclean thing can dwell with God," and because we are all unclean—owing to our many weaknesses and transgressions—Mormons believe that, were it not for the Lord Jesus Christ, mankind would have no hope at all.

Mormons consider Jesus Christ to be the Savior of all mankind, and that His merciful Atonement and suffering for the sins of each and every person on earth (if they take advantage of His gift by repenting) satisfies the law of justice, and washes away all uncleanness, thus permitting our eventual return home . . . to dwell with God in heaven. They believe that Christ's Atonement opened the door to repentance and the remission of sins, and that His Resurrection opened the door to immortality, eternal life, and exaltation.

INDEX

Humanitarian Service, 91
Humility, 108, 159
Humor, 45, 51, 52, 84
Husband, 51, 91, 128, 131, 136, 199
Husbands and Wives (see also
    Marriage), 57, 105, 110, 111,
    122, 123, 131, 188
Hymnal/Hymn Book, 85, 98, 193
Hymns, 98, 129, 192, 193, 211

Immersion, 157, 162, 163, 168, 182
Immorality, 62, 103, 104
Immortality, 151, 169, 213
Infants (see also Babies), 94, 201
Infidelity, 121, 123
Inspiration, 22, 51, 144, 147
Interview with the Bishop, 134, 146,
    199, 200
Isaiah, 11, 53, 172
Israel, Tribes of, 18, 33, 131

James, 76, 164
Jehovah (see also Jesus Christ), 5, 10,
    11
Jesus Christ, 7, 10, 13, 17, 18, 20,
    22, 23, 24, 29, 33, 34, 42, 43,
    48, 62, 65, 66, 69, 73, 75, 77,
    80, 82, 103, 108, 114, 128, 129,
    132, 136, 138, 143, 144, 145,
    146, 150, 151, 152, 153, 154,
    155, 157, 158, 159, 161, 162,
    163, 164, 165, 166, 172, 173,
    174, 175, 177, 180, 182, 184,
    186, 189, 190, 191, 195, 199,
    202, 203, 205, 207, 213
Advocate with God the Father, 9,
    162
Author of Repentance, 202
Firstborn of the Father, 171
Jehovah, 5, 10, 11, 171
Jesus of Nazareth, 1, 5, 8
Lamb of God, 17
Lord, 8, 11, 14, 17, 20, 60, 78,
    81, 151, 152, 153, 159, 162,
    167, 168, 173, 175, 194, 198,
    206, 213
Only Begotten Son of the Father,
    17, 48, 162, 181
Savior, 1, 8, 11, 36, 68, 78, 151,
    153, 162, 199, 213
Son of God, 1, 2, 5, 6, 8, 23, 66,

77, 143, 150, 151, 168, 182,
    183, 213
Jews, 1, 14, 17, 27, 31, 33, 34, 35,
    50, 53, 103, 121, 131, 138, 157,
    169, 186, 194, 195, 204
Jobs (see also Employment), 60, 72,
    87, 100, 127, 128, 136, 145,
    200
John, 18, 162, 163, 186
John the Baptist, 146, 182
Joining a Church, 5, 16, 21, 25, 29,
    31, 35, 36, 38, 39, 43, 46, 47,
    62, 63, 65, 66, 67, 76, 77, 89,
    102, 110, 125, 148, 154, 159,
    173, 187, 210
Joseph and Mary, 171, 212
Judah (one of the Twelve Tribes of
    Israel), 33, 34
Judaism (see also Jews), 33, 131
Judgment, 128, 153, 154, 164, 165,
    175
Just/Justice, 62, 90, 164, 165, 175,
    186, 187, 213

Kennedy, John F., 50
Kimball, Spencer W., 43
King James Version of the Bible, 10, 49
Knight, Gladys, 41

Laman/Lamanites, 14
Latter Days, 17, 77, 143, 144
Law of Moses, 17, 34
Laying on of Hands, 146, 168, 183
Lay Ministry, 141, 147
Lehi, 14, 15, 53
Lieberman, Joseph, 50
Life after Death, 90, 131, 151, 153,
    161, 168, 181, 186
Local Congregation, 36, 60, 66, 86,
    87, 92, 112, 130, 134, 135, 136,
    137, 138, 139, 140, 141, 146,
    147, 148, 182, 189, 192, 193,
    194, 196, 197, 198, 208
Lord, The (see also Jesus Christ), 26,
    81, 157, 206
Lord's Prayer, The, 191
Love/Loving, 62, 65, 74, 75, 90, 108,
    122, 128, 155, 164, 175, 187,
    190
Lucifer (see also Satan), 171, 172,
    173
Luke, 155, 172, 212

ABOUT THE AUTHOR

W. F. Walker Johanson lives in the Virginia suburbs of Washington, D.C., with his wife, Kerry, and the youngest of their five children. In addition to being the at-home mother of five, Kerry is an accomplished professional artist, with special expertise in paper, clay, and multimedia sculpture, and is a graduate of Thomas Edison State College. Their oldest son, Nils, served his two-year mission in Rosario, Argentina, is a graduate of The University of Virginia, and is in law school at The University of Michigan; their next oldest daughter, Cooper, graduated from Brigham Young University in Art, and is living in Salt Lake City, where her husband, Ben Burgess, is finishing his degree at The University of Utah (they have a wonderful daughter, Addie, and a new son, Nolan); their next oldest son, Håkon, has just returned from his two-year mission in São Paulo, Brazil, and is resuming his college work at Brigham Young University in Business; their next oldest daughter, Riley, is also a student at BYU, studying Painting in the School of Visual Arts; and their youngest daughter, Carson, is just starting high school.

Having been raised in the Presbyterian, Congregationalist, and Methodist traditions, Johanson joined the Mormon Church as a convert, just one month before his thirtieth birthday. Since becoming a member, he has served as a bishop, as a member of a stake presidency, as a high counselor, as a public affairs director, as a stake mission president, as a Gospel Doctrine teacher, and in dozens of other lay positions in the Church.

Johanson is a graduate of The University of Michigan, and has been the president of The National Institute for Organizational Research, a national marketing and communications consulting firm, for twenty-eight years. He is an expert in higher education marketing, having served as a consultant to nearly three hundred college and university presidents across North America . . . and is an accomplished marketing strategist, writer, and public speaker.